THE JEWISH MOTHERS'
HALL OF FAME

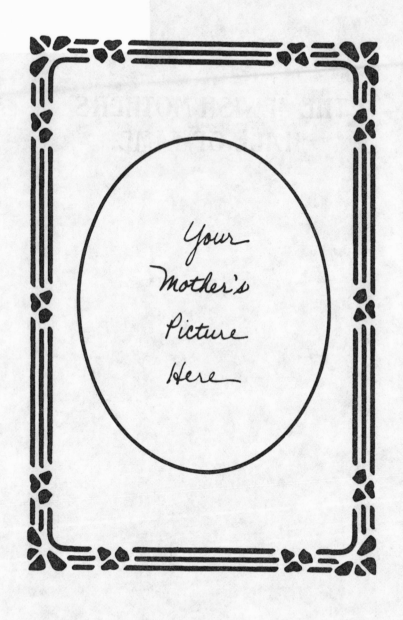

*Your
Mother's
Picture
Here*

THE JEWISH MOTHERS' HALL OF FAME

by
Fred A. Bernstein

A Dolphin Book

Doubleday & Company, Inc.
Garden City, New York
1986

Library of Congress Cataloging-in-Publication Data

Bernstein, Fred A.
  The Jewish mothers' hall of fame.

  "A Dolphin book."
  1. Women, Jewish—United States—Interviews.
2. Mothers—United States—Interviews. 3. Jews—
United States—Interviews. I. Title.
E184.J5B495 1986   973'.04924   85-24541
ISBN 0-385-22377-9

Printed in the United States of America

To my mother

Contents

Foreword by Lisa Birnbach

I can tell you about Jewish mothers because I have one. (Oh, didn't you know? Yes, I am.) I also have a Jewish father. And brothers. Cousins. (Our dog may be; I never checked.)

Being a Jewish mother means more than just being a Daughter of Zion with children. It means much more than simply ushering in the Sabbath Queen. It is more complicated than only redistributing guilt. It's harder than cooking brisket.

It has to do with participating in a legacy of histrionics and love-smothering, medical school applications and gym excuses (and my favorite note of all time: "My daughter Lisa has permission to use my credit card today"). It has to do with great humor and *kvelling*.

Jewish mothers are only nominally like normal mothers. A Jewish mother would never have "left it to Beaver." Why give up total control? Besides, no Jewish mother that I've met has ever waited until her husband came home from the office to vent her opinions. They're feisty even during business hours.

Of course not all Jewish mothers are alike. Once, when I was about nine, my mother put a heap of Breakstone sour cream in a bowl. She told me she had *made* me sour cream for lunch. On the other hand, my grandmother, Ruth Salit, was a famous feeder who believed that a "sliver" of food was any morsel smaller than, say, the landmass of Burma.

I know some Jewish mothers who don't look Jewish. There has even been some debate over whether to be a JM it is absolutely imperative to be J. If I only had a nickel for everyone who has confused "concerned" with "Jewish."

Why the defensiveness? Because I know sooner or later I will be one too.

Even if my own mother, Naomi Birnbach, had not been selected for *The Jewish Mothers' Hall of Fame*, I would still recommend this book. Fred is a very good writer, has excellent manners, went to Princeton (around the time they had quotas, if you know what I mean), and is one of the very few young men I've met through my mother that I've liked. Lord knows she's tried.

Preface

Baseball players have their hall of fame. So do fly fishermen, graffiti artists, and sushi chefs. But there has never been a hall of fame for Jewish mothers—until this one.

Why create a Jewish Mothers' Hall of Fame? Because behind every successful man or woman is a mother who has sacrificed, supported, and protected.

Because when Steven Spielberg wanted to film blood oozing out of *someone's* kitchen cabinets, guess who volunteered? His mother, Leah, bought thirty cans of cherries, then she cooked them until they exploded all over her kitchen.

Because when Neil Sedaka wanted a piano, his mother, Eleanor, took a job as a bra model.

Because when Abbie Hoffman had to live as a fugitive from justice for seven years, his mother, Florence, sent him toothbrushes through secret underground couriers, with notes reminding him that dental hygiene is important.

Jewish mothers are just like any other mothers, only more so. They want their sons and daughters to be rich (only more so) and famous (only more so) and happy (only more so).

The mothers in this book are just like any other *Jewish* mothers, only more so. These are the mothers whose children are already rich and famous and (hopefully) happy. In some cases, they made great sacrifices to help their children get ahead. Others merely held on for dear life as children who seemed destined for great things got busy.

How hard is it to make this hall of fame? There are about 2 million Jewish mothers in America (not counting all the ones who aren't even Jewish!). But there are only 65,000 places in

American medical schools (and only 3,000 of those are in the Ivy League). Each year, there are only 23 Oscars, 71 Grammys, and 6 Nobel prizes waiting to be claimed. (As for sainthoods—forget it.) Tough odds for even the most determined Jewish mother.

What awaits mothers who beat those odds? The Jewish Mothers' Hall of Fame.

In 1981, while I was interviewing Gene Simmons, the leader of the rock group Kiss, for a magazine article, we paid a visit to his mother on Long Island. In her foyer, Florence had hung a banner that read WELCOME HOME, MY DARLING ONLY SON. In one spare bedroom was a radio tuned to a station that occasionally plays Kiss; Florence *never* turns it off. Three other rooms had been turned into a Kiss museum, full of gaudy memorabilia. I was amazed by Florence's devotion. Then I heard about the hardships she had overcome to raise the darling only son who became a rock star, and I realized Florence would make a great story.

A few months later, at a kosher dairy restaurant in Beverly Hills, I met the owner, Leah Adler, who is Steven Spielberg's mother. Leah turned out to be the funniest person I had ever met. When I asked her if she knew, when Steven was growing up, that he was a genius, I expected her to say, "Of course." Instead she answered, "When Steven was growing up, I didn't know what the hell he was." I had found another great interview subject in Leah Adler.

With Florence and Leah for inspiration, I set out to find other mothers like them. I wrote letters; I made phone calls. All told, I spent two years interviewing the twenty-five women who make up this first, official, Jewish Mothers' Hall of Fame.

Actually, when I began the book, I thought it would take three months to complete. No mother, I figured, would warrant more than a couple of pages. Instead, the mothers turned out to be more interesting, more insightful, and more diverse than I ever imagined. The result is a book many times longer, and I hope many times more interesting, than I originally thought it would be.

Acknowledgments

Every one of the mothers in this book devoted time and energy to helping me become a published author, and for that I am in their debt. Equally important, none of them attempted to control what I could write about them. As a journalist, I know how rare that is, and I am deeply grateful.

Many others helped in the preparation of this book. I am particularly thankful to my past and present agents, Peter Heller and Suzanne Gluck, for getting the project off the ground, and to Paul Bresnick of Dolphin Books for guiding it successfully to publication. Throughout, Cutler Durkee and Merle Feld provided valuable editorial advice.

For favors large and small, and for encouragement and friendship, I would also like to thank: Bernard Adler, Joan Antelman, Carl and Chris Arrington, Elizabeth Bernstein, Lisa Birnbach, Dr. Joyce Brothers, Iris Burton, Andrea Chambers, Robert Cohen, Eddie Feld, Harvey Fierstein, Lois Fitton, Lisa Frost, Uri Geller, Mitch Golden, Hilliard Goldman, Richard Gordon, Dan Greenburg, Bill Henry, Alita Hernandez, Abbie Hoffman, Holly Holden, Alison Holtzschue, Betty Lee Hunt, Karen Jackovich, John Katzman, Fran Lebowitz, Johnna Levine, Marilyn Michaels, Meyer Mishkin, Marvin Mitchelson, Robin Platzer, Maria Pucci, Harry Reems, Steve Reidman, Marilyn Rifkin, Rory Rosegarten, Patricia Ryan, Dotsie Salituri, Neil and Leba Sedaka, Ira Schreck, Lynn Seligman, David and Vicki Sheff, Barbara Shelley, Debra Sherline, Gene Simmons, Carol Wallace, Irving Wallace, Rosalyn Yalow, and the husbands of all my mothers. (Guys—I promise I'll get you in the next book!) Above all, I would like to thank my father, Milton Bernstein.

THE JEWISH MOTHERS' HALL OF FAME

Steven Spielberg's mother

LEAH ADLER

"I DIDN'T KNOW HE WAS A GENIUS. FRANKLY, I DIDN'T KNOW WHAT THE HELL HE WAS."

The restaurant could only be in California: shingled on the outside, kosher on the inside, it is the unlikely domain of Leah Adler, a petite blond godsend whose responsibilities include planning the menus, greeting the guests, and whenever her son has a new movie out, hanging the posters.

The movie posters—nine so far—are Leah's way of telling anyone who doesn't know it that her son is Steven Spielberg. Four of the ten biggest-grossing pictures of all time—*Jaws, E.T., Raiders of the Lost Ark,* and its sequel, *Indiana Jones and the Temple of Doom*—are heralded on Leah Adler's wall. Also represented there: *Poltergeist, Close Encounters of the Third Kind, The Goonies, Back to the Future,* and *Gremlins,* which together make Steven the most popular filmmaker ever.

Leah is right to show off. Among the reasons for Spielberg's success are his incredible energy, his un-selfconscious sense of humor, and his youthful, wide-eyed innocence—qualities which he clearly inherited from his mother. Visiting Leah at the Milky Way, I feel as if I am meeting the inspiration for a thousand Spielberg movies. Leah projects the same rapturous naïveté as Steven's protagonists as she ricochets from table to table, joyously igniting conversations in every corner of the room. And when the phone rings, Leah positively leaps across the room to get it.

"The most important thing in my life is my restaurant," says Leah, who Steven describes as having "more energy than a hundred mothers." "It's like a stage. I feel like I'm opening in a play every night. I thrive on the whole thing."

From the looks on their faces, Leah's customers do too. Not surprisingly, the restaurant is a smash. How does Leah know that? "Even Steven Spielberg," she jokes, "can't come without making a reservation."

"I didn't totally understand *Close Encounters,*" admits Leah as she settles into a booth in a corner of the restaurant. "But *Jaws* I liked better. At one point, I heard somebody in the theater screaming at the top of her lungs—and then I realized it was me."

Practically every day, someone at the restaurant—often someone who mistakenly addresses her as "Mrs. Spielberg"—asks her if she always knew that Steven was a genius.

Leah has an answer ready: "When he was growing up, I didn't know he was a genius. Frankly, I didn't know what the hell he was. I'm really ashamed, but I didn't recognize the symptoms of talent. I did him an injustice. I had no idea back then that my son would be Steven Spielberg.

"For one thing—and he'll probably take away my charge accounts for saying this—Steven was never a good student. Once, his teacher told me he was 'special'—and I wondered how she meant it.

"You see, Steven wasn't exactly cuddly. What he was was scary. When Steven woke up from a nap, I shook." Long before *Gremlins,* Steven was a master at creating terror. He practiced on his three kid sisters. Says Leah, "He used to stand outside their windows at night, howling, 'I am the moon. I am the moon.' They're still scared of the moon. And he cut off the head of one of Nancy's dolls and served it to her on a bed of lettuce.

"The first thing I'd do when we moved to a new house was look for a baby-sitter," Leah says. "But it didn't work, because they wouldn't let us go out for more than a few hours without taking Steven.

"Once," Leah remembers, "I took Steven to the Grand

Canyon. He said, 'This is nice,' and then he threw up. With Steven, you held on for dear life.

"I mean, I didn't know how to raise children," Leah continues. "Maybe we were more normal than I remember—but I sincerely doubt it. Steven's room was such a mess, you could grow mushrooms on the floor. Once his lizard got out of its cage, and we found it—living—three years later. He had a parakeet he refused to keep in a cage altogether. It was disgusting. Once a week, I would stick my head in, grab his dirty laundry, and slam the door.

"If I had known better," she says, "I would have taken him to a psychiatrist, and there never would have been an *E.T.*"

Leah is only kidding. "We had a great time," she says. "We really did. I loved when the new toys came out. I couldn't wait to get them home."

How did Leah get to be so "up"?

"I don't think you can cultivate these things," says Leah. "An up person is always up. You get it from your parents.

"Mine was not a conventional childhood at all," Leah continues. "For one thing, my mother and father were madly in love with each other their whole lives, and I thought that's how everybody lived."

Leah's mother, Jennie Posner, was a public speaker. "When they opened a building, they'd hire her to speak. She had a speaking voice like a singing voice. I remember her walking around the house, practicing her speeches while she dusted. She mostly missed the dust—she was never too domestic. She was a marvelous lady who never mastered the can opener in her whole life."

Leah's father was no more down to earth. Philip Posner, a Russian immigrant, never earned a living, but that's not what Leah remembers. "My father was so exciting," she says. "I have memories—color memories—of walking through a snowstorm in Cincinnati. It was glistening, and he looked up and said, 'How wondrous are thy works.' " Leah is teary-eyed. "How wondrous are thy works. This is who I am. This is who Steven is."

Philip's family included a brother who was a Yiddish Shakespearean actor. "I remember him in the living room doing 'To

be or not to be' in Yiddish." Another brother, Boris, was a
vaudevillian—"he used to dance with a straw hat and a cane.
Later, he became a lion tamer in the circus." Officially, Leah's
father was in the shmatte (clothing) business, but what he really
liked to do was dance ballet and play guitar. "He was so creative," Leah sighs, "and beautiful to look at.

"We were poor," she adds, "but there was no depression in
our house. We didn't know what we didn't have. And we liked
what we did have. I remember going to bed thinking, 'Wow, I
have new shoes,' and jumping out of bed in the middle of the
night to look at my new shoes. Now that I can have everything,
I've lost that."

Leah remembers a time when the family barely ate for
several days. Finally, her father was able to earn ten dollars
buying and selling old jewelry. "He came home with the ten
dollars and said, 'We're going on a vacation.' And we did. That's
faith."

Life gave Leah another advantage. "I was different-look-
ing. But I never wanted to change. If I had had a tiny pug nose,
maybe I wouldn't have had to develop a personality. But instead, I learned to play piano. I was somebody. I loved my life,
and I believed in me."

Leah studied to become a concert pianist, but she gave up
that ambition when she married Arnold Spielberg, an engineer,
and moved with him from Ohio to Scottsdale, Arizona.

She also moved away from her religion. Though Leah was
raised in an Orthodox home (and she embraced Hasidism when
she married second husband Bernard Adler), she chose to raise
her children in a Gentile neighborhood. She calls that "my one
really big mistake.

"The kids next door used to stand outside yelling, 'The
Spielbergs are dirty Jews. The Spielbergs are dirty Jews,' " Leah
remembers. "So one night, Steven snuck out of the house and
peanut-buttered all their windows."

Leah indulged him. "I was never a typical parent," she says.
"I think if a kid wants something, he ought to have it."

Once Steven wanted a job painting a neighbor's tree trunks
white. Reports Leah, "He did three trees; guess who did the

rest? And once we asked him to paint the bathroom. He did the toilet and the mirror, then he quit."

Leah's mother saw something she didn't. "My mother always used to say, 'The world is going to hear of this boy.' I used to think she said it so I wouldn't kill him."

Steven became even more demanding after he joined the Boy Scouts and signed up for a Merit Badge in moviemaking. Steven's father bought him a Super-8 camera. Reports Leah of her house, "The decor from then on consisted of white walls, blue carpeting, and tripods."

When he wasn't shooting at home, Steven would take the family on location. "My car back then was a 1950 Army surplus jeep. We would load it up and drive into the desert. Steven had the whole family dressed up in ridiculous costumes. He'd say, 'Stand behind that cactus,' and I actually did it. I also supplied the cold cuts."

When he was fourteen, Steven made his first full-length movie, a sci-fi flick called *Firelight*, and he got a theater in Phoenix to show it. It was Leah who put up the letters on the marquee. "I thought, 'This is a nice hobby.' " Incredibly, the film made money, and there was no stopping Steven. Once, Leah says, "he wanted to shoot a scene in a hospital, and they closed down an entire wing. Another time, he needed to shoot at an airport, and they gave him a whole runway. Nobody ever said no to Steven. He always gets what he wants, anyway, so the name of the game is to save your strength and say yes early."

At least once, she should have said no—early. Steven wanted to do a scene (similar to one in *Poltergeist* twenty years later) in which something horrible came oozing out of Leah's kitchen cabinets. She not only agreed but went to the supermarket and bought thirty cans of cherries, which she cooked in a pressure cooker until they exploded all over the room. "For years after that," she jokes, "my routine every morning was to go downstairs, put the coffee on, and wipe cherries off the cabinets."

Her routine changed dramatically after she divorced Arnold Spielberg, settled in California, and fell in love with Bernard Adler. (When I ask her how long she and Adler have been married, Leah says, "Not long enough.") Seven years ago, they opened the restaurant together, and together they spend more than twelve hours a day there. "For it to be kosher, an Orthodox Jew has to be here at all times," explains Leah. "We really go home just to sleep."

And for shabbes. "By two o'clock on Friday," she says, "I'm ready to collapse. But shabbes is a restorer." Most Saturdays, the Adlers take part in a Hasidic service in West L.A. "Everything looks different on shabbes," she says. "Everything glistens."

Everything glistens in Steven's world, too. At eighteen, he began hanging out at Universal Studios, pretending to have a job there. Soon he did. At nineteen, he sold his first script, and with the proceeds he bought a TV for his mother. There have been many other presents. Says Leah, "He spoils me rotten, like I spoiled him. Of course, I buy him beautiful presents, too, but I charge them all to him."

Now that Steven is a mogul, the only thing that's changed, Leah says, is "you can't expect him to come to dinner every time you invite him." But when he does come, they have "normal family conversations. I say, 'Hi, Steven,' and he says, 'Hi, Ma, what's for dinner?' When he's scoring a movie, he calls and says, 'Come over, we need your musical advice.' It's a crock, but I love hearing it. He's very family-oriented."

Last year, Steven gave Leah a bit part in an episode of *Amazing Stories*, his TV series. "I was the only extra who ever got a limousine," jokes Leah. During breaks in shooting—some of which lasted hours—Leah hung out in Steven's office. According to Leah, he said, "I love coming back and finding you here. Could you come more often?"

Another time, Leah says, she got a call from Steven's secretary. "Steven is sick," she said, "and he wants you to make a pot of chicken soup. We'll send a limousine to get it." Leah, who was at the Milky Way, said, "Steven knows this is a dairy restaurant and I can't make chicken soup here." Five minutes later, Leah says, the secretary called back and said, "Steven says, 'Go home and make it.' "

Did she? "Of course," says Leah. "No one else makes Steven his chicken soup."

Leah is equally devoted to her daughters: Nancy, who's in the jewelry business in New York ("When she comes out, we steam up the diamond cases at Neiman-Marcus"); Susan, a mother ("She puts her creativity into raising her two children"); and Anne, a screenwriter ("She's paying rent and eating and everything these days"). "I don't feel I own these kids," says Leah. "It's not that they're reflecting me, or that I'm living vicariously through them. It's just that I really like them."

Leah's one regret is that her parents didn't live to see Steven fulfill his dreams. "Every time I get into a limousine, I want to say, 'Hi, folks, look at me.' But Steven always says, 'Don't worry, Ma, they know.'"

In that case, they know how much fun Leah is having. "I get all the glory," she says, as she walks past one of Steven Spielberg's movie posters. "I eat it up. And all I have to do is be the mother."

Dan Greenburg's mother

LEAH GREENBURG

"You've been here three hours. Do you think
I'm anything like the mother in the book?"

The building looks like hundreds of others along Chicago's Lake
Shore Drive, but it is not. This is a sacred place, the Mount Sinai
of Jewish Motherhood disguised as a white-brick luxury high-
rise. For it is here that the law was revealed unto Dan Greenburg, who titled his commandments *How to Be a Jewish Mother*.

The difference between Dan and Moses is that Greenburg
couldn't get *his* Torah published in stone, so he settled for soft
covers. It's just as well. Since 1964, the book has sold 3 million
copies in fifteen editions. A generation of Jewish mothers
learned how to be exactly how they've always been—but more
so—from Dan Greenburg. And I was finally, in this tower of
white brick, going to meet his maker.

So it was with the fervor of a pilgrim that I ascended, by
elevator, to Leah Greenburg's apartment. Until then, everything I knew about her I had learned from her son's book. There
was, for instance, the "Foreword by the author's mother," in
which Mrs. Greenburg admitted:

"I haven't actually read what he has to say here, but I'm
sure it's very pleasant if he wrote it. You'd think that it wouldn't
be such a hardship on a young man who writes so nicely to write
an occasional letter to his mother, but it seems there are more
important things to a young man these days than his mother. All

right, never mind. I only hope you will like the book and I pray that the whole experience has taught him something."

Dan's "mother" was only warming up. The next ninety-or-so pages of *How to Be* revealed a matriarch who:

Told her teenaged son, "You won a Pontiac automobile in the youth group raffle? Very nice. The insurance alone is going to send us to the poorhouse."

Practiced, in front of a mirror, her delivery of the line "I'm fine, it's nothing at all, it will go away."

Served bread with everything:

"Irving, wait. Take a little bread with that."

"Bread? With strawberry ice cream?"

"Just a little piece. To help wash it down."

Saved empty Bufferin bottles:

"You may buy Bufferin someday when they'll be out of bottles."

Told her daughter:

"All right, maybe I've been too critical. Is it a sin to want only the best for your children? What I am saying is this: Maybe it's not so important you should marry only a professional man. Your father, after all, was in ladies' buttons. So if you should come across a nice young fellow and you should fall in love with him, and if he should also be in love with you, and if—may the good Lord not burn out my tongue for saying this—if this young man should not be a college graduate . . . all right, I say go ahead and marry him! By that time, your father and I will probably both be dead anyway."

That just had to be Leah Greenburg talking. Dan Greenburg couldn't be that good a writer.

"These are all very funny things," says Leah, who is small and white-haired, "but it's a composite of many mothers. You, as a writer, should understand." She is looking through Dan's book for the first time in years. "I don't know where he got these things," she chuckles. "It's amazing how a person's imagination can work."

She reads aloud the mother's plea to her unmarried daughter. "I mean, was Sam, my late husband, in ladies' buttons?" No. And while we're at it, did Dan ever win a Pontiac in the youth group raffle? No. And did Leah ever make him eat bread with strawberry ice cream? No—well, maybe. "He needed to put on weight," Leah recalls. "So we did kind of insist that he eat bread. Dan as a boy was always sick with something, and the doctor said, 'Before I take his tonsils out, fatten him up.' He was my first child, and the first child you pay more attention to."

Now we are sitting at the dining table, eating homemade blueberry cake with Leah's good silver ("Don't worry; it gives me a chance to use it"). When the book came out, she remembers, "some of my friends were offended—they knew the mother in the book wasn't like me. The ones who didn't know me, of course, wondered. I was at an Oneg Shabbat and people kept saying, 'Are you really like that?' I said, 'Dan interviewed a lot of mothers for the book. It's you, and you, and you'—I pointed to every woman there.

"A friend of mine, who was Irish, was more of a Jewish mother than me. When her son got married, she was so worried he wouldn't get the breakfast she made for him that she called him every morning—on his honeymoon. Do you think I would do anything like that?"

Now we are walking around the apartment, admiring the work of Sam Greenburg, a talented painter who died in 1980. A Chicago native, Sam traveled to Paris in the twenties to study art. Leah, who was born in Kovno, Lithuania, to a wealthy dry goods merchant, was at the Sorbonne when they met. "He was a fine boy, with a degree and a Phi Beta Kappa," she remembers of Sam. "We were married in Paris—such a romantic place. It was a simple student wedding. Then we lived in Cairo, where Sam did cartoons for a newspaper, and then we spent some time in Palestine before Sam took me home to Chicago."

The Greenburgs sailed into New York Harbor on Black

Friday, 1929. "Here we were, coming to make a living, and people were jumping out of windows." In Chicago, things were not much better, but Sam found work as a substitute teacher. (He eventually became a supervisor of art education for the Chicago schools.) Leah began working as a Hebrew school-teacher, her profession for the next thirty-seven years.

But her real career was raising her two children. Dan, who came along in 1936, was never interested in sports, she recalls. "He was a quiet, introspective boy. He was an artist. He used to make clay figures that were perfection. But he wasn't a bad writer, either. When I meet his teachers on the street, they tell me they will never forget his writing."

Still, Leah was surprised by Dan's success. The first time she read *How to Be a Jewish Mother* (including the foreword, which Dan had written for her), she secretly wondered who would buy it. Later, when the book took off, "I was flabbergasted. Evidently, it appeals to a lot of people."

Leah is one of those people again, now that she has a reason to leaf through the book. "You forget how many funny things there are in here. Of course, he took certain liberties. You've been here three hours. Do you think I'm anything like the mother in the book?"

It's time for me to leave now. "When are you going to eat again?" Leah asks. "On the plane? How can a boy like you go until eight-thirty at night without having a meal?"

Three times she asks me if I want a nice turkey sandwich. Three times—thinking I've overstayed my welcome—I say no. And then, somehow—I don't know how—I am sitting at Leah Greenburg's table, good silver and all, eating a nice turkey sandwich.

I should have known Dan Greenburg's mother wouldn't let me down.

❧ Lisa Birnbach's ❧
mother

NAOMI BIRNBACH

"IF THERE WERE AN EGG BANK, I'D WANT LISA TO DONATE EGGS."

In 1980, Lisa Birnbach told her mother, Naomi Birnbach, that she was writing a book about how to be a preppy. Recalls Naomi, "I thought, 'That's cute. It won't sell, but maybe it will be good exposure for Lisa.'"

Naomi—also an aspiring writer—was happy to help out. So she penned a short essay called "I Gave Birth to a Preppy." It appears on page 16 of *The Official Preppy Handbook*. I've agreed to reprint part of that essay here. I'm doing this strictly as a favor to Naomi. (I mean, she was obviously right when she said nobody would want to read about preppies.)

I Gave Birth to a Preppy
by Naomi S. Birnbach
(Abridged by Fred A. Bernstein)

One year after marriage, I gave birth to a baby girl. I was looking forward to a blissful mother-daughter relationship, but my tiny offspring immediately began to assert herself in very distinctive ways. She flatly refused Pampers and demanded 100 per cent cotton diapers. She didn't play house; she played cottage. While the other little girls lavished attention on their baby dolls, my daughter pretended to find a baby-sitter for hers.

Yes, the first five years with my daughter have been quite an experience. I am certainly going to miss her, but she is determined to go off to a good boarding kindergarten. She's busy going through the catalogues now. . . .

So how have the two writing Birnbachs fared since all that *Preppy* stuff was published? Lisa watched her handiwork climb to the top of the best-seller lists, where it remained for twenty-two weeks. She appeared on every major talk show, in dozens of newspapers and magazines, and on almost a hundred college campuses across the country. While traveling from school to school, she began collecting data for *The Lisa Birnbach College Book*, which in 1984 made her a best-selling, critically acclaimed author once again.

Naomi, meanwhile, has authored press releases for a case management firm, written short stories for a black teen publication, and sent several proposals off to *Mad*—one of her favorite magazines since the days when her children read it. "I've done a lot of weird stuff," admits Naomi. "Mostly, I've collected rejection letters, all of which begin, 'Dear Sir or Madam.' "

But Naomi, like the aspiring writer she is, turned her dejection into the subject of more writing. She cranked out a piece about her blocked career path, part of which is published here for the first time:

Where Did I Go Right?
by Naomi S. Birnbach
(Abridged by Fred A. Bernstein)

Success isn't what it's cracked up to be, especially when it's my daughter's, and most especially when it's in my chosen field.

I graduated from college, frantic to write for television. I wanted to win friends and exact tributes. I craved recognition as a thrust against those who were unkind—I'd show them one day. Or maybe I would write a book of witty, original observations and then be forced by a clamorous public to become a media personality. The fantasies were drawn in fine detail. But they never made it into reality. Shelving career plans as did many of my generation, I retired to marry and produce this daughter and her brothers. . . .

This lovely, soft child of mine has realized her ambitions and mine too. The success of her book has mandated public appearances.

Now life becomes confusing. I walk down the street and expect to be recognized, and am—the dry cleaner says, "Saw your daughter on TV last night." The line between us blurs. I wrote to a friend, "Our book has just come out." "Our?" Who was on television last night—she or me? She looks like me and she talks like I do—or vice versa.

We older kids got sidetracked back there. After the diploma and the training program, there was the inevitable typing test. Suddenly, being a wife and mom seemed a more meaningful destiny. Wasn't that what we were here for?

The daughters, however, are out there reporting the news, suing unequal opportunity employers, curing our ills, and curling our hair. We can only cheer them on, with pride shining in our eyes and dripping down our faces, past a faded smile as we watch them —sometimes on TV—succeed. We who started the dream see it fulfilled in them. Ah, mixed emotions.

Eventually, Naomi came up with a plan for finding meaningful employment, and, she wrote an article about that, too.

Nepotism: Or What to Do When Your Kids Won't Hire You
by Naomi S. Birnbach
(Abridged by Fred A. Bernstein)

I have some work experience—if you consider sitting on panels of homemakers who indicate their detergent preferences "work experience."

My last long-held, paying job was in 1977. From January 12 to February 9.

From marriage on, I had a long, mostly boring history of volunteer work. I also joined the brigade of itinerant course-takers, taking everything from "Basic Architecture" to "Automobile Tune-up"—and we don't own a car. The worst part was when I noticed the professor was my son's age and had forgotten to button up his jacket.

Oh, to enter the job market and be gainfully employed.

In my view, nepotism is an offshoot of the commandment: Honor thy mother and thy father. What greater honor can one perform than: put thy parent to work?

All industries are expected to hire minority applicants when feasible. Hiring a mother will fulfill most antidiscrimination requirements.

Remind your child of your competence and skills. You have proven ability to research, type, scream, and sew costumes.

What you're up against is your children's fear that your old-fashioned and mother-like ways will embarrass them, plus some residual hostility from the past, when you were boss. So, assure them that, if hired, you will not take their temperature if they sneeze or recommend heavier clothing in front of their secretaries. Propose a contract that calls for immediate dismissal if you remark "Sit up straight" once during a board meeting.

If all else fails, try adopting—maybe an executive recruiter.

I first met this funny woman on a freezing February afternoon. Lisa escorted me to her mother's home, in an elegant Upper East Side building. The vast apartment looked like something out of, well, the *Preppy Handbook*.

"The living room in the book is this living room," Naomi tells me. "That grandfather clock has been in my family since I was a child. Everything here was inherited. The furniture isn't dusty—but it could be. And I haven't painted in eight years. I like things to be done properly, but not spit-and-polish. I'm definitely a preppy housekeeper."

It must seem like I've come to inspect Lisa's prep pedigree. Naomi continues: "We belong to a club; but it's so low-key that I only wear my old clothes. I've always liked B-squared [that's Preppy-talk, I learn, for Brooks Brothers]. And during the day I wear no jewelry at all, because I think it's in poor taste."

Naomi is, indeed, dressed down. But with her well-scrubbed face and lustrous brown hair, she looks like she could be her daughter's sister, and I say so.

Naomi isn't buying. "I just ran into somebody I knew from high school. And she said, 'Naomi Salit, you haven't changed a bit.' And I said, 'You mean I had gray hair and wrinkles in high school?' "

But when I say that she and Lisa act like sisters, she agrees.

"We're very clony about each other," says Naomi, who calls her daughter Lu.

Both possessors of retentive minds and lilting speaking voices, they career from one wildly funny bit of conversation to another.

The subjects range from Lisa's old boyfriends . . .

Naomi Birnbach: Just picture Charles Manson.

Lisa Birnbach: He was a brilliant physicist.

NB: And what really bothered me was that he already had a girlfriend.

. . . to Naomi's feet

LB: Tell Fred about your feet.

NB: I have the best middle-aged Jewish feet. If I ever met a foot fetishist . . .

A few months later, Naomi and I arranged to meet for lunch. Naomi, who had just come from getting her hair done ("I call it crisis intervention"), nibbled on a plain hamburger while we talked.

Fred Bernstein: There were so many questions I didn't get to ask last time. When the *Preppy Handbook* came out, did people think that Lisa was trying to pretend she wasn't Jewish?

Naomi Birnbach: We understand that some people have said that. But nobody who knew us even superficially would think for a second that we would try to pass. We are so strongly identified with Judaism. When Lisa was at Brown, there wasn't a teacher on the campus who didn't know that Lisa Birnbach went home for the Jewish holidays, that she didn't eat pork or shellfish, that her father had been in the Irgun. You couldn't be more Jewish than we are.

FB: Are you religious?

NB: We are very observant in comparison with many people. The house is kosher. Friday night is sacrosanct—the kids, when they're in town, are always expected on Friday night, and I'm usually rewarded. And the boys and Mr. Birnbach go to synagogue practically every Saturday. One of my sons wrote an essay in which he said about his father, "We didn't play catch together. We didn't do Little League together. What we did was walk to synagogue together." It was very moving. A lot of my husband's generation practices its religion by rote. But Mr. Birnbach understands law, and reason.

FB: But you seemed so proud of your preppy apartment.

NB: We think it's the best of both worlds. It's unusual for people to be as Jewish as we are and still be so admiring of Greenwich, Connecticut style. But I got it from my parents, and I must say I think Lisa picked it up from me.

FB: What's Mr. Birnbach like?

NB: Mr. Birnbach—I call him Uncle Maks—is an amazing man. He's biblical, truly biblical. The children adore him—and they weren't brought up to.

FB: Tell me about him.

NB: Maks has an incredible life story—I can't do it justice. He grew up in Frankfurt, Germany, where his father had a prosperous department store. In 1937, someone wrote on the house, "Jew go to Jerusalem." My father-in-law said, "Not a bad idea." Two weeks later, forty-seven members of the Birnbach family pretended to go to the countryside for a picnic. Enjoined not to talk to each other—so they would not appear to be a family—they got on a train, leaving the lights on in the house, and left Germany forever. They told the maid, whose name was Betty, "We'll be home for dinner." From Trieste, my father-in-law called his office. He learned his head bookkeeper had just killed himself, on the grave of his mother, and left a note blaming "the Jew Birnbach." The point is, if they had delayed even one day, my father-in-law would have been arrested.

FB: What happened then?

NB: The family settled in Palestine, where they remain to this day. Maks joined the Irgun. In 1948, Menachem Begin sent him to America to raise money, arms, and consciousness for the Irgun. Mr. Birnbach couldn't speak English, but he did remarkably well at raising tremendous amounts of money. And once he was here, he decided to remain here. In Israel, he had been exporting gems to the U.S.; now he decided to import what he had been exporting.

FB: Tell me about your family.

NB: My father was a conservative rabbi—Norman Salit. He is still well known; the generation has not yet died that knew his name.

FB: What was your childhood like?

NB: The biggest event was my sister's death. When Mimi was sixteen, and I was in college, she developed a whole set of bizarre symptoms. A year later, she died. The closest determination was encephalitis. In terms of my being a parent, there's no question that it was a tremendous factor. It made me a hypochondriac. I wanted to have everything biopsied. The nose runs, I want to take the kid to the doctor. I dissipate more energy in sheer panic. . . .

FB: Did you try becoming a writer after college?

NB: I had a very demanding father. He had such high goals, I think I was so scared of failing, that I didn't try. If it had been an expectation, I might have felt more encouraged—but as a demand, it was intimidating. I don't feel I ever lived up to my potential.

FB: And then you met Maks. . . .

NB: At a dance. Our sense of humor corresponded right away. He used to call me a Birnbach in a skirt. We had fun; we still have fun.

FB: What were your ambitions for your children?

NB: I remember thinking, because my father was such a genius, that whatever my shortcomings were, I was going to produce superb children. They could be as neurotic as hell, they might not be able to get along with other children—but they would be brilliant.

FB: Was Lisa brilliant?

NB: She read voraciously. But I remember one of her teachers saying, "Lisa will be a slow developer. It will take her a long time before she learns to write well." But she was always funny. Lisa would come home from school and say not "I got good grades today" but "I was funny today." It was important that they have a sense of humor.

FB: Was she a difficult child to raise?

NB: She was so beautiful and so good and so no trouble and so no sweat. She raised herself.

FB: She was never rebellious?

NB: Her biggest act of rebellion was when she got her hair permed, in 1977. I hated it—with a burning passion. There was also the time she wanted to live in Washington in a house with two boys. I went down there to make sure they lived the way I wanted them to—the two girls upstairs and the two boys downstairs. I thought living together meant four in one bed.

FB: Do you miss her now that she's on her own?

NB: Absolutely. I sometimes think we shouldn't have nagged her to get a job—if we hadn't, she'd still be living at home, which we'd love.

FB: Did you expect the *Preppy Handbook* to be a success?

NB: No. No way. I thought, "She won't make any money this year. We'll have to help her out."

FB: How did it feel to be proven wrong?

NB: I was awed by Lisa. It's not just writing—she's dynamite at communicating. I can't sing "The Star-Spangled Banner" in a stadium with thirteen thousand people without trembling. And there she was on TV. I used to call everyone I know. The pride is unharnessable.

FB: Were any of your friends jealous?

NB: No. Well, maybe one or two. And there were some people who thought all the publicity was really tacky. But mostly it's been good.

FB: Were you jealous of your daughter's success?

NB: If jealous means that I wanted it to be me, not her, no. But that I want some of it for me, yes. It would have been lovely if I had some. But in a million years I wouldn't have denied it to her. Because I adore her, and because she includes me in her life. I don't feel like a second-class citizen in Lisa's life.

FB: Did her success help your career?

NB: Well, I used her name when I wrote to *Mad*—I guess it didn't help.

FB: What don't you like about Lisa?

NB: Nothing. I get excited about Lisa—I get excited about all my children. But of course, the report cards aren't in till they pick mates.

FB: What if she doesn't?

NB: If she said she didn't want to get married? I would be heartsick. It would take a lot of years to reconcile myself to that. I would feel that she was deprived and I was deprived.

FB: But Lisa is one of the most successful writers of her generation. Maybe she can't have everything.

NB: Then I would wish her half of her success to trade off for a marriage. Maks says he would rather have a baby than a new book. I want Lisa to have a marriage more than I want her to have a career.

FB: Why?

NB: It's a reflection on my own marriage. I don't think anyone's life can be complete until they're with another person. And I have selfish reasons. I want her married because I want to know someone's looking after her. When I can't find her, I want to be able to call someone and say, "Where's Lisa?" My fantasy is that from the day she's married, I can relax.

FB: What about children?

NB: She must have a kid—or three. I want it for Lisa, I want it for me, and I want it for the Jewish people. You know how terribly important that is to me—the survival of my race. But mostly, I want there to be a perpetuation of Lisa. I want more Lisas. If there were an egg bank, I'd want Lisa to donate eggs.

FB: She's that terrific?

NB: Sometimes, on the street, I see lines of Dalton School girls, and I look at them and say to myself, "How are you going to grow up, little girl?" And then I think, "You could never grow up more beautifully than my little girl. You couldn't do better than to turn out like my Lisa."

Eddie Fisher's mother

KATE STUPP

"HE WAS A GOOD, FINE BOY. THE BEST. HE JUST HAD
A LITTLE BAD LUCK ALONG THE WAY—ABOUT
GETTING INTO THE WRONG MARRIAGES."

Eddie Fisher's mother cries a lot these days.

She cried the last time she heard Eddie sing "My Yiddishe
Mama," because, "When he sings it, I know he's singing it for
me."

She cried while watching Eddie record his last album. "The
men in the studio kept saying, 'What's wrong?' And I said,
'Nothing. These are tears of joy. He hasn't made a recording in
fifteen years.' "

She cried when she read Eddie's autobiography, *My Life,
My Loves.* "I could only read a couple of pages a night," she
recalls, "because I cried so much."

Those weren't tears of joy. Eddie's book chronicles perhaps
the most pathetic fall from glory in the history of entertain-
ment. In the fifties, he was the preeminent popular singer in the
world; just over a decade later, he was virtually unknown except as the butt of humiliating jokes. Along the road to igno-
miny, Eddie Fisher was divorced four times (from Debbie
Reynolds, Elizabeth Taylor, Connie Stevens, and Terry Richard, a twenty-two-year-old Miss Louisiana whom he married at
forty-eight), he gambled his way into bankruptcy, and he spent
twenty years as an amphetamine addict. He carried around

suitcases full of hypodermics, and he injected himself before every show.

"Whatever happened to him, she did to him," says Kate. The "she" is Elizabeth Taylor. Kate is serving me her home-made pound cake ("I don't buy, I bake") in the living room of her North Philadelphia apartment. And she is breaking her promise to herself not to talk about Eddie's exes.

"She made him suffer so much—such a good boy."

Perhaps she is talking because she knows that, thirty-five years after he became a star, Eddie Fisher is still remembered as the man Elizabeth Taylor dumped for Richard Burton. Or perhaps she simply needs to get something off her chest.

"It isn't what she did," declares Kate, now eighty-two. "It's how she did it. The others were all different.

"When Elizabeth Taylor meets a man, she takes him and squeezes the life out of him and then she throws away the pulp.

"When he married her, he was sincere. He really loved her. But I don't think Elizabeth Taylor knows what love is.

"How many has she had now? Eight? Believe me, it won't be the last one. I can't stand her.

"Of course, she still didn't go back—she's still Jewish. That's a wonderful side of her.

"I'll tell you who the divorce really hurt. Elizabeth's mother. She took it so bad when they broke up. She loved Eddie. He was an ideal husband for her daughter. I think she's a sick girl.

"Of course, I didn't know anything. My Eddie never talked to me about it. He doesn't tell me because he doesn't like me to worry about anything. He's such a darling, my Sonny Boy.

"I always call him Sonny Boy, like in the Jolson song. Even in front of the President, that's what I called him.

"I think there's times when everyone's unhappy. But when I see my Sonny Boy, he's always happy.

"When he introduced me to each wife, I liked her as a person. The only thing I asked, with each one, is if they loved each other.

"Of course, I have opinions about all of them, but it isn't my place to talk. They were all nice to me. They all called me Mama.

"With Debbie Reynolds, I felt very bad. I thought this was going to be a good life.

"When I met her, I said, 'Debbie, my child, I love you. I want you to be happy with my Eddie. Let me tell you something and I won't bother you again. Give a little, take a little, and you'll always be happy.'

"Of course, it didn't work out. Who knows what goes on behind closed doors.

"I'm not a prying mother. I didn't ask the children if they were having difficulties. I could never do that—not with any of my seven children.

"Eddie never cried on my shoulder. He was no weakling, my Eddie. He could have been concealing things—but believe me, he never said an unkind word about his wives.

"But he's still close with the kids. His children are so nice, and they're so close with their daddy.

"I saw Carrie at her wedding [to singer Paul Simon]. There were a lot of famous people there—I can't tell one from another. But I wanted to see Debbie and Eddie's children—Carrie and Todd.

"Of course, I'd seen Carrie as Princess Leia—it was great. It was the second movie. The first one, Eddie didn't like. He said, 'You don't have to go; she'll do another.'

"She's so cute, and so nice. At the wedding, she put her hands on my face, and she said, 'Is this what I've been missing all these years?' And Paul [now Carrie's ex] is such a nice young man. But show business is a very hard life." Kate is showing me pictures of the wedding, sent to her by Maxine Reynolds, Debbie's mother.

"He has two little girls with Connie; they come to his shows. He's crazy about them. He loves the children.

"My Eddie and Connie are still very good friends. She's very nice. I guess they found some reason to divorce.

"He always married big names, but it didn't end good.

"He was a good, fine boy. The best. He just had a little bad luck along the way—about getting into the wrong marriages.

"That part was bad, but thank God he came out of it all right.

"He always says he's the black sheep of the family. He's not. He's a wonderful Sonny Boy."

> One of these days, when there is time, I hope to meet someone to whom I can show the wonderful things I have discovered and see her starry-eyed with the same kind of excitement I feel. I think she'll probably be a home girl rather than one from show business. Most of all I want her to have Mom's kind of common sense.
>
> —Eddie Fisher in *The American Weekly*, 1953

Before he met Debbie, or Elizabeth, or Connie, or Terry, there was only one woman in Eddie Fisher's life. He had begun crooning a string of twenty-two hit songs—songs like "Oh! My Pa-pa" and "Lady of Spain"—that would earn him more than $1 million a year. There were crowds whenever he appeared in public. Rona Barrett, then a teenager named Rona Burstein, was the president of Eddie's fan club. "We controlled more than a million girls," she said. "I thought he was God's gift, and so did all the others."

But even gifts from God need to have mothers. So Eddie, who was still single, kept Kate, who was divorced from Joseph Fisher, at his side. The newspapers showed her fixing Eddie's tie backstage, helping him pack before he went on tour, enjoying the house he bought for her in Philadelphia. And the captions—dictated by RCA Victor publicists—elevated Kate to the level of folk heroine. They were the perfect American couple: Eddie and his devoted Yiddishe Mama.

> The best thing that ever happened to me was my mother. Even when my six brothers and sisters were wearing second-hand clothes, she never told me to stop singing and get a job. "Singing is what you're

made for, Sonny Boy," she said. "Keep it up, and you'll get there."

—Eddie Fisher in *The American Weekly*

The daughter of a penniless immigrant tailor, Kate Minicker had married young—and badly. "It was a hard life with Mr. Fisher," she says. "He was a good man, but there were problems."

Kate is too polite to talk about those problems, but in his book Eddie recalls, "My father took his anger and frustration out on my mother, shouting at her, insulting, ridiculing, and humiliating her. He never beat her physically. The way he beat her mentally was worse. He was a tyrant who treated my mother like a slave."

Eddie adds, "I wanted my mother to fight back, and because she never did, I thought she was weak. Now I realize she was the strongest of us all."

Maybe she couldn't fight back; Kate was too busy trying to raise seven kids in shacks with bedbugs and rats and no hot water—and packing up the whole household and moving when she couldn't pay the rent. An itinerant luggage repairman, Joseph Fisher was reduced by the Depression to hawking rotten vegetables—and part of what little he earned, he lost playing the numbers.

> Some of the time, we were on relief, and Mom would stay up all night to unravel the things the welfare agencies gave us and knit new clothes.

—Eddie Fisher in *The American Weekly*

College was out of the question for Kate's children. But Eddie had another meal ticket: "When he opened his mouth, you couldn't believe what came out of it," says Kate, "and from such a little boy."

By the time he was eleven, Eddie was singing at the family's synagogue in South Philly. When the cantor got sick, his mother recalls, "they put him on a box and he did the whole service. I cried and cried.

"But then the cantor came to the house, and he said, 'Don't let him become a cantor; you don't get anywhere.' If he hadn't said that," Kate intones, "Eddie would be a cantor."

Instead, he began winning one amateur contest after another, and soon he was singing regularly on a children's radio program.

> His mother used to give him four pieces of cardboard every morning. They were to cover the holes in his shoes. One set was for the morning and the other set was a change for the afternoon. . . . He used to walk the four miles, back and forth, to the station.
>
> —The New York *Post*, 1953

Finally, Kate, desperately worried that Eddie would ruin his voice without proper instruction, barged into the office of a renowned vocal coach. She convinced him to see Eddie for free. "He said, 'Young man, are you willing to give up baseball and playing in the snow? Because you'll have to if you want to sing.' And Eddie said, 'Yes, yes.'

"Show business was a tough nut to crack, but that's what Eddie wanted. I really didn't think he would make it," Kate says. But she never told him that during the three years he spent scouring New York for work. He didn't find it.

> Eventually, I went home feeling all washed up. I just hung around the house. Mom would keep saying, 'Why don't you call up Mr. Blackstone [a promoter],' and I'd say, 'No, Mom, I've had it.' One day she told me, 'You're young, Eddie. Discouragement is a disease. You're young.' I went back to New York.
>
> —Eddie Fisher in the *Daily Mirror*, 1955

Eventually, Milton Blackstone got Eddie a job—headlining at the Riviera Club, in Fort Lee, New Jersey. Kate, who was preparing for one of her daughters' weddings, nonetheless raced to the theater to be with him.

> Just before the show Mom came into my dressing room and for once in her life she was more nervous than I was. But she gave me a bright smile. 'You've done it before, and you can do it again,' she said.

> The lights went out except for the spots and I felt the music stirring inside me. Mom had always told me, 'You can do anything when you have the will for it.'

> Her life was the proof. I remember her on her knees washing the stones that paved our little back-yard so we kids could have a clean place to play. . . .

> —Eddie Fisher in *The American Weekly*

Kate's pavement-scrubbing days were over. In 1949, Eddie Cantor heard her son sing at Grossinger's and predicted, "Within one year, this man will be a star." Says Kate, "I can still see him saying those words."

Within a year, Eddie *was* a star. And Kate had another reason to be happy. According to Eddie, she had always told her husband, "I am going to divorce you as soon as the children are older," and she kept her promise. Then she married Joseph's best friend, Max Stupp, whom she calls "an angel from heaven. We had a perfect life together."

Eddie lavished presents on his mother, but he saw her less and less. Indeed, his memoirs make it sound as though he saw her only at his weddings. Eddie wrote, "Ties to my family began to disintegrate about the same time everything else was falling apart." Eventually, he even stopped sending his mother money. "There came a time," he wrote solemnly, "when my generosity had to be reserved for my pusher."

> Sonny Boy is what Mom and Dad have called me
> for as long as I can remember. Maybe that sounds
> corny, but none of us will ever change.
>
> —Eddie Fisher in The New York *Post*, 1953

By the early sixties, Sonny Boy had changed. Kate was at Philadelphia's Latin Casino when Eddie—after waiting for a drug delivery backstage—came on two hours late, to a terrifying chorus of boos and hisses. Soon he was reduced to playing small clubs overseas to earn money for narcotics.

Kate's luck ran out, too. After sixteen years of marriage, Max Stupp died. Then her daughter Nettie, who was left retarded by a childhood injury and had always been Kate's closest companion, succumbed to cancer. Eddie remembers, "I thought that would kill her, but she survived. Mom always survives."

She moved in with another of her daughters. But after a year Kate announced, "I want to go back where I belong."

Now she lives with Dora Schaeffer, who used to be her next-door neighbor, in a two-bedroom apartment.

"Any of my kids would gladly take me in. But I don't want to interfere," says Kate.

"My Eddie wanted to build me a home in California, but I said, 'No, I want to stay here.' I said, 'Sonny Boy, let me stay here where I started.'

"He did everything for his mommy. They all did.

"An interviewer said to me, 'What's it like having a star for a child?' And I said, 'Which one? I have seven stars.' Every one's a star in his own right.

"I raised seven children in real hardship, but I raised fine children. The way they turned out, every one a beauty! I have eighteen grandchildren, and four great-grandchildren—the oldest one is fifteen. They call me Bubbe.

"I'm rich. I'm so rich. My bedroom is all pictures. They're beautiful, and they're as good as they are beautiful.

"You feel they're around. To an old mother, that keeps her going. I have a phone in this room, and a phone in the bedroom

—and they keep ringing all the time. I just spoke to Eddie. He calls me every other day.

"My mother always said, 'To make good bread, you've got to have good dough.' You've got to have something to work with.

"Nowadays, you've also got to be very lucky. I wouldn't know what to do to raise my children in this time. They start adult lives so young—by the time they come of age, they're tired of their lives. Years ago, it had to be really bad before they got divorced. Not now.

"My children went to Hebrew school—you can't make them go now.

"But each generation is different—you've got to go along with it. I have eighteen grandchildren, and when their parents tell them what to do, I never say a word.

"I come in contact with a lot of mothers who interfere in their children's lives. My friends, they'll say, 'My daughter went away, and she didn't take me.' I could disown them as friends when they start complaining about their children. That's not the way I do it. If my daughter says she's going away, I say, 'Have a wonderful time.' That's their life. Is that being a bad child?

"My friends say, 'You're a lucky mother. But you deserve it.' "

Kate's doctor doesn't let her fly. "But whenever Eddie performs in New York or Atlantic City—anyplace I can go by limousine," she says, "I go. And every song he does is great. Now I'm talking like a mother—like a mother should."

The high point of the show? When Eddie sings "My Yiddishe Mama." Kate, who always sits in the front row, cries, just as she cries when she listens to the song on a cassette that she keeps at her bedside. She plays it almost every night.

"I just want a little more time with my children," Kate says, playing the song for me. "I'm so proud of them, every one of them.

"I know I'm being greedy. But God should give me just a little bit more time."

Adam Rich's mother

FRANCINE RICH

"ONCE, ADAM SAID TO ME, 'MA, WHEN AM I GONNA BE A STAR?' IT MADE ME FEEL VERY GOOD THAT HE DIDN'T THINK HE WAS ONE."

When Adam Rich was five, his mother asked him if he wanted to be on TV. "Okay," he said, "but how do I get in the box?"

The answer, in his case, was talent. The first time Adam Rich tried out for a commercial, he was hired. In fact, he was hired for more than twenty-five commercials (including spots for McDonald's, Pillsbury, and Chevrolet) by the time he was seven. Then he was chosen to play Nicholas Bradford, the baby of the family in the hit series *Eight Is Enough*. For four and a half seasons, Adam stole the show, which garnered top ratings for ABC and won millions of fans for the shaggy-haired actor. He also earned about as much per week as most kids would make in a lifetime of shoveling driveways.

That was bound to cause problems for Adam's parents—and it did. When I visited the Riches at their home in Chatsworth (in the almost-rural northern San Fernando Valley), Adam's father told me:

"When he first started in the business, I was jealous. Here I was, a mechanic—and I'd been working twenty years—making around a hundred and fifty bucks a day. And do you know what I had to do for that money? Then Adam comes along and does a commercial that takes half an hour, and he gets twenty-five thousand dollars. You can imagine how that felt."

Rob and Fran, sweethearts since they were in high school together in Bensonhurst, Brooklyn (they moved to California in 1968, six months after Adam was born), eventually came to terms with his success. Indeed, she says, "I think we're closer now because of it. But we were lucky. I know a lot of famous children with divorced parents, and often the divorce happened soon after the child became successful."

The four-foot eleven-inch Francine faced up to many other problems. For the first two and a half years that Adam was on TV, she accompanied him to the set every morning. It was tough gaining acceptance. "There's an image of a stage mother," she says, "and people stay away."

But Francine made them like her. In 1978, *TV Guide* did a story on Adam. The reporter noted that the actor's mother "wins popularity contests on the set for being cooperative, agreeable and good company."

But Francine wasn't through. She still had to learn to:

- Cope with the sometimes frightening crowds that formed around Adam in public.

- Convince old friends not to be jealous.

- Teach Adam the value of money, in the face of his astronomical income.

- Manage that income.

- Teach Adam the difference between acting and real life.

Did she succeed? The *TV Guide* story concluded, "All Adam wants out of life now is his own spaceship and the *Star Wars* robot R2-D2 to live with him forever. But if he's really smart, he'll sign his mother to a lifetime contract."

During the two hours I spent with Francine in her kitchen, Adam, who was sunning himself by the backyard pool, made only one appearance. He looked in the refrigerator, which was jammed with food, announced disgustedly, "There's nothing to eat in this house," and left. But as he did, he turned to me and said, "She's a good mother."

After hearing Fran's story, I know.

" So much depends on the parents.

" When Adam first started in the business, I had nobody to turn to. I know I made mistakes.

" Since then, I've sometimes thought about becoming a consultant. I have helped many parents in the same situation.

" Once, Adam said to me, 'Ma, when am I gonna be a star?' It made me feel very good that he didn't think he was one. We've tried real hard to keep him level-headed.

" I don't know where he gets his talent. He was named for my great-grandfather, Aaron Feller, who was in vaudeville. But there are no other performers in the family.

" He certainly didn't get it from me. I get butterflies just doing an interview, like now. I'm doing it, but I don't like it.

" Last week, I had to speak before the PTA—I'm head of the drug and alcohol abuse committee—and I thought I was going to have a heart attack.

" But that's not Adam. He's always been a very confident person. He was talking in complete sentences at eighteen months. People would stop us wherever we went. He just had a great personality. Finally, my grandmother said he might be good on TV. Until she said it, I had no idea.

" When he was five, I saw an ad for kids who wanted to be in commercials. The first commercial he went on, he got. And every other one he went on, he got too. I guess he just has something about him. But I really don't know what. My husband and I have always asked ourselves that question.

" When he was seven and a half, he tried out for *Eight Is Enough.* I asked him if he was nervous at the audition. He said, 'Why should I be?' He got the part.

" At first, a neighbor cared for Wayne, who is five years younger than Adam, while I was on the set. What people forget, when they hear about how much money he made, is that the kid really worked: he got up at five o'clock every morning. And we never knew when we'd be home for dinner. It was hard for Adam.

" There were other problems, too. At first, he'd get confused between the series and real life. He'd bring the situation from the show home with him, and he'd try to pull it on us. You'd think there were eight children in this house. He would try to get out of being reprimanded by acting really cute. And he could cry whenever he wanted to, because he had to learn that for the program.

" Once, we shot at a school, and three hundred people mobbed him; I thought he was going to be crushed. I can be neurotic, like anyone. You worry about your kids nowadays, anyway. But you're doubly worried when someone's in the public eye. There are a lot of nuts out there—we've gotten people knocking on the door at midnight.

" In the show's third season, I hired someone to be his guardian, so I could spend more time with Wayne, and also work.

" I'm a receptionist at a college dorm. I answer the phones, I do clerical work, I do a lot of things to help the students. People say, 'I can't believe you're Adam's mother. You're so down-to-earth.'

" A lot of my friends don't understand why I work. But I do it for my self-esteem. I need to have my own identity. I'm not just Adam Rich's mother.

" I also do volunteer work. I'm chairman of my neighborhood watch, and I'm the den mother for my younger son's Cub Scouts. And then there's the PTA—I head up the drug and alcohol programs. It involves a lot of work.

" I'm a very concerned parent. I'm really your typical Jewish mother.

" The hardest thing I do is manage Adam's money. It goes into trusts for him. We have it tied up, so when he's eighteen, he won't be able to spend it foolishly. That's the real reason I do it.

" It's not that I don't want him to enjoy it. But we know kids who blew it all as soon as they turned eighteen. Everything in moderation, that's what I say. You can't tell a kid, 'The world's a candy store; buy anything you want.'

" When he was younger, and he wanted a very expensive bicycle, we told him he had to save for it. We still say no to Adam. We recently said no to a trip he wanted to take to Tahoe. And we said no when he wanted an ATC—that's an all-terrain cycle—because he already had a motorcycle.

" We try to live just like an average family. We don't consider his earnings our earnings. We've had so many other rewards. We've gotten to travel all over. When we were in Washington, we got VIP tours everyplace. You couldn't ask for more.

" Adam still gets an allowance—twenty dollars—and Wayne gets five dollars. Just like any other family. And Adam gets yelled at, just like the other one gets yelled at.

" He's a good kid, but he does get spoiled. When Adam goes into a store, they get so excited, and they say, 'Anything you want, you can have.' I think that's wrong. Kids lose their sense of values that way. It's really up to the parents.

" One Hanukkah, he got over a hundred presents. We told him he could pick a few he liked, and the rest he gave to charity.

" We're just trying to teach him responsibility, but it's hard.

" After being in prime-time television, if you talk about somebody making thirty thousand, forty thousand, even a hundred thousand dollars a week, that sounds normal to him.

" Also, I don't want him to think that money is power. I don't believe it is, and I don't want him to feel that he can buy friends.

" It's hard for him. Once he came home and said, 'I don't know who my true friends are.' It's confusing. I said to him, 'It takes time. You'll figure out who they are.'

" Fame can be scary for Adam. When we first moved into the neighborhood, he was the local celebrity. One night, a gang of kids followed him home on his bicycle. He came in and said, 'I think they want to kill me.' My husband went outside, and they said, 'No, we just want his autograph.'

" It always amazes me that no matter where we go, he's recognized. We were in Spain, and he must have signed four thousand autographs in forty-five minutes. Sometimes, he says he *isn't* Adam Rich.

" But he likes it when gorgeous blondes come up to him. He even got to meet Farrah when he was little. She said, 'What's your sign?' and he said, 'Jewish.'

" Now he goes to a regular school. But he used to have school on the set. We were lucky: There was a teacher who made it interesting. But he didn't like school then, and he doesn't like it now. He's a B student. Give him recess anyday.

" For his bar mitzvah, we had a private tutor. We managed to keep the whole thing private, which was wonderful, because there were a lot of famous people there.

" Right now, he's good friends with Ricky Schroder. But most of his friends aren't in the business. He's really a regular Joe. He's a sports nut, like his father. And of course he's counting the days until he gets his learner's permit.

" He still goes on auditions. But he's at an awkward age. When he gets rejected, sometimes he cares and sometimes he doesn't. But maybe it's just as well—he's getting a taste of what being a normal kid is like. Although we feel he's always had a normal life.

" Since he first started in the business, we made a point of telling him that it might not go on forever—that most child actors aren't actors as adults. We thought it was important for him to understand that. And we want him to know that there are other options out there.

" Last year, he wanted to be a baseball player, then a hockey player. Now he wants to be a rock guitarist. But I'm sure he'll stay in the business in one way or another.

" Wayne was an actor, too, from the time he was six. We wanted to give him the same opportunity that we gave Adam. But he didn't enjoy it. So he retired at seven.

" Wayne's more interested in politics now. He wants to be the first Jewish president, and I think he'll make it.

" He's very proud of his brother, but I wouldn't say he's jealous. Wayne and Adam fight, but you can tell that there's a love between them.

" Of course, when Adam first made it big, some of our friends were jealous. You could feel the jealousy. People wonder: Are you going to become a snot? Are you going to show off? Are you going to buy everything in sight?

" But now they know we haven't changed. We still have the same friends, although we've met a lot of terrific people in the business.

" I have to say, for us, the whole experience has been fantastic."

David Brenner's mother

ESTELLE BRENNER

"THE WHOLE FAMILY HAS A SENSE OF HUMOR EX-
CEPT ME. GIVE ME A JOKE AND I'LL DO SOME-
THING TO RUIN IT."

David Brenner was a mistake.

"When you have two grown children, and a baby on the
way, it's a mistake," explains his mother.

Estelle Brenner was past forty when she found out she had
a baby—David—on the way. Her daughter was a teenager; her
son was twenty-three. And times were hard.

Estelle tried to abort the fetus. One doctor had her "take
pills so big I could hardly swallow them." But when she went
back to the doctor, he told her the "mistake" was hanging on for
dear life.

The doctor said, "Medically, it shouldn't be here. Perhaps it
has an important reason to live."

Her best friend said, "Have the baby. It'll keep you young
when you're old."

Lou, her husband, said, "Leave it alone; something good
will come of it."

Estelle decided to have the child. "And from that moment
on," she says, "I never had a second thought. Because I love
children—and David was a joy to raise."

Until 1969, David Brenner was a TV documentary producer. Then he decided to try to make a living telling jokes. As
his friend Joan Rivers puts it, "He dared to give up the stature,

the money, and the medical plan to walk onto a stage and take a chance." David's gamble paid off. He quickly graduated from the comedy-club circuit to the high-priced showrooms of Atlantic City and Las Vegas. On TV, he has done more guest spots (according to *The Book of Lists*) than any other entertainer.

And so, forty years after Estelle decided to give David life, he's returning the favor. "He makes every day a happy day," she says. "He makes us want to live."

I met the Brenners at a hotel in the Catskills, where David had arranged for them to spend the summer. Lou, who's eighty-eight, greeted me in the lobby. "I don't know what's wrong with these people," he told me, referring to the other guests. "They get sick when it's time to start living."

Estelle was no less jovial when I met her in their room. A talented amateur painter, she is gradually losing her eyesight. She told me, as I faced her across a small table, "I can see you but I can't make out your features." But she is thankful for a lot of things—including a husband who still adores her after more than sixty years of marriage. Lou reads to Estelle practically every night (their favorite book is David's *Soft Pretzels with Mustard,* about his childhood in Philadelphia). And when they travel, he videotapes everything they see. Then he shows her the tapes on a large-screen television, which she watches with her special telescopic glasses.

Estelle reminds him that she didn't need videotapes to appreciate Israel, which they visited for the first time last year. "When I set foot on the ground," she says emotionally, "I felt a tremor."

Lou: "They were having an earthquake that day."

Then, too, Estelle is thankful for her son and daughter, who are both retired, and her four grown grandchildren, who call and visit all the time.

But David! "There is nothing in this world he wouldn't give me," says Estelle. He has bought his parents apartments in Florida and Atlantic City, and cars, and jewelry (most of which

David designed). "Look at this," says Estelle, showing me a ruby bracelet that her son created. "I never take it off."

Last winter, David sent his parents on an eighty-seven-day around-the-world cruise. They barely had time to change their clothes before they headed for the Catskills. Says Estelle, "Who would think all this would happen to us? I wouldn't have any of this luxury if I didn't have such a good son."

But it's more than jewelry and trips. "He's given me such happiness," says Estelle, who has seen David perform hundreds of times. "He does nothing off-color, never. You can take a child. That's why people like him. All I ever hear is, 'We love your David.' You can imagine how that makes me feel."

Estelle has tasted celebrity herself. She and Lou have appeared with their son on over a dozen TV shows. True, people usually ask for Lou's autograph, not hers—perhaps because Lou looks so much like David. But Estelle got her revenge on *Donahue*, when she said, "I know I'm David's mother, but Lou I'm not too sure of." The audience cracked up.

That was a new experience for Estelle. "I always tell her not to try to repeat any of David's jokes," says Lou, "because she'll ruin his reputation." Estelle agrees: "I'll start in the middle, or I'll give away the punch line first. The humor, it's all from Lou. The whole family has a sense of humor except me. Give me a joke and I'll do something to ruin it."

"Okay," I say. "You're on." I ask Lou for a joke.

He says, "One day, I was walking down the street, and I grabbed a woman's pocketbook. Then I started to run, and the police came, and they were chasing me. So I jumped onto a scale and got *aweigh*."

Then I ask Estelle to repeat it:

Estelle: "I was walking down the street, and somebody grabbed a pocketbook . . ."

Lou: "You're wrong already. Let me tell it."

Estelle: ". . . and I ran down the street."

Lou (snoring): "You left out 'the police were chasing me.'"

Estelle: "Oh, yeah, the police are chasing him, and so he jumps onto a scale and gets *aweigh.*"

Lou: "She got it right, but only because I corrected her. If I didn't correct her, *gevult.*"

Estelle Rosenfeld was born on Manhattan's Lower East Side. Her immigrant parents spoke Yiddish. Estelle didn't always understand them, and, she says, "I'm not sure they understood each other." The family moved to Waco, Texas, where her mother's stepfather had a general store. Estelle remembers traveling by steamboat to New Orleans, then by train to Waco. There were no other Jews in Waco.

There was also no work in Waco for her father, a coatmaker. So when Estelle was twelve, the family moved to Philadelphia, where a few years later she met Lou Brenner. The son of a prominent Orthodox rabbi, Lou had been a vaudevillian during World War I, but he had given up performing publicly in deference to his father.

Lou never stopped cutting up in private. Estelle remembers of their first date, in 1919, "He was funny and spontaneous, just like now."

Estelle is going to describe that date, but Lou says, "I might as well tell it, because she doesn't remember."

Lou goes on, "Well, I showed up in spats and a derby; I looked like someone out of an old gangster movie. And I bought a big ten-cent cigar. On the stoop, I lit up the cigar, and then I rang the bell. When she came to the door, I said, dramatically, 'I am your admirer.' Then I nonchalantly tossed the cigar into the street." Later, he bought her a box of candy for the extravagant sum of thirty-five cents. He gave the merchant a dollar and told him, "Keep the change."

Says Lou, "I had to make a showing. I was twenty-three; it was time to get married."

The date went well, so well that, after he dropped Estelle off, Lou picked up the cigar in the street, wiped it off, and put it in his pocket. He figured, "I can use it again on the next date."

He also returned to the candy store and demanded his sixty-five cents back.

There was a second date, and Estelle starts to tell me about that one. "He was so funny. I introduced him to a girl, and she sat down on his hat and flattened it like a pancake."

Lou: "What did she say? What did she say? You've got to get the joke in there."

Estelle doesn't remember.

Lou: "She said, 'I'm glad I met you,' and I said, 'Yeah, well I'm not.' That's what makes it funny."

After they married, Estelle's cooking was more grist for Lou's mill.

Lou: "When we got married, she didn't know nothing about food. I told her I wanted lox, so she went to a hardware store."

Have you heard the one about the liver? It was so dry, Lou says, that he nailed it to the sole of his shoe and refused to take it off. Or the one about the chicken that Estelle forgot to clean? "Actually," defends Estelle, "I partly cleaned it." But she admits, "I had no interest in cooking. I loved to paint—I was an artist, and I was much better at that. That was my interest, instead of staying in the kitchen." Now she jokes, "It's my gain, because Lou has to take me out."

They could barely afford to eat in when David came along. And he didn't like her cooking, either; Estelle remembers that David especially dreaded her mashed potatoes. "He said they had lumps. He said everything had lumps, even my chicken soup. Usually he didn't eat them, but one night, he cleaned his plate. I kept saying, 'David, you're such a good boy. Such a good boy.' Then the next day, I went to wash his pants, and what did I find in them? The mashed potatoes. You've never seen such a mess."

I ask her what she did about it.

"I laughed. That's how you get along when you don't have any money."

So what if she can't tell a joke? Much more important for David, she never stopped him from being funny.

There were times she wished she could have. One childhood picture shows David nonchalantly eating the feather on his mother's favorite hat. "There were so many practical jokes," says Estelle, "that it got to the point where I was afraid to wake up on April Fools' Day. But he would look at me with those big brown eyes and that smile, and I could never be angry at anything he did."

His teachers weren't so forgiving. David was constantly getting kicked out of school—and Estelle was constantly having to write excuses—until David thought of a solution. He told Estelle his class was doing a project in handwriting analysis, and he needed her signature on the bottom of a couple of dozen sheets of paper. Then he used them when he needed them; Estelle insists it wasn't until years later that she found out.

"Even now, David is always full of surprises," Estelle says. "But they're always nice surprises; the kind that make you happy. He's always giving us parties, or flying friends or family in to see us."

Of course, Estelle would love for David to get married. "He doesn't have the time," she says. "I'm not sure it would work." But she is certain he'd make a good husband.

Estelle once told him, "If you become half the man your father is, you'll be twice the man any woman would ever want or need.

"I always gave my children an awful lot of love and respect," says Estelle. "I'm very fortunate that I'm getting so much in return."

Dr. Joyce Brothers' mother

ESTELLE BAUER

"YOU PROBABLY WANT SOMEBODY WHO'S HAD
TRAGEDIES. WHO WANTS TO LISTEN TO A GOODY-
GOODY?"

When I reached Estelle Bauer by phone at her New York apartment, she was baking apples. "You caught me being a cook. My granddaughter—Joyce's daughter—is coming in tomorrow," she explained. "I want to give her a good meal."

When I told her the reason for my call, Estelle agreed to talk ("the cooking can wait till the morning"). But she warned me that she would be a boring interview subject. "I'm just a good girl. You probably want somebody who's had tragedies. People love to read horror stories. Who wants to listen to a goody-goody?"

I took my chances, and for more than two hours we talked about her life, her famous daughter, Joyce, her not-so-famous daughter, Elaine, her four grandchildren ("I don't think of them as grandchildren; they're grown people already"), and her three great-grandchildren. "I'm surrounded by love," she said. "So whatever comes, illness, this goes wrong, that goes wrong, it doesn't matter. I'm bolstered up. You don't find many people who have it that way."

You sure don't. Each week, Dr. Joyce Brothers receives thousands of letters from troubled people. Every day, she answers a few of them in her syndicated column, which appears in newspapers in over a hundred cities.

I read Estelle some of the questions that Joyce has answered in her column in the last few months, and Estelle responded. (Her answers appear below.)

But again she had a warning: "There's no way I can be as smart as Joyce. She has such a fund of knowledge. She has rooms full of articles. Her staff has everything filed and counterfiled. I'm just speaking as a mother."

"Sounds good to me," I told her.

Dear Dr. Brothers' Mother:

I'm a suburban housewife and mother who should be very happy, but I'm not. I hate myself for being full of envy and jealousy even though I have a beautiful home and a good husband who loves me. I have few women friends because I can't seem to keep from making snide comments. I'm getting sick because of these emotions.

—A.B.

Dear A.B.: Find something you are good at doing, and become an expert at it. It will make you feel better about yourself, and less inclined to envy others. You will have something to talk about other than your jealousies, and you will stop being your own worst enemy.

Fred Bernstein: What's it like having a famous daughter?

Estelle Bauer: Well, to tell you the truth, after so many years, I take it for granted. I can't follow all of Joyce's activities. I just know if I turn on the TV, she'll be there.

FB: What do you think when you see her?

EB: I make sure she looks okay. I make sure her hair looks right. I'm her biggest critic.

FB: Are you close?

EB: Very. We have a funny relationship. I start to say something, and she says, "Mother, I've already thought of that," before I even finish the sentence. We understand each other so well—we just click.

FB: You never fight?

EB: We have never had to argue. There have never been any mean words. As I said, I'm not an interesting person. You've got the wrong party.

> Dear Dr. Brothers' Mother:
>
> My 12-year-old son has a very high IQ, but he scores rather low on creativity. How could this happen? His father and I are interested in the arts and we were hoping he'd enter some artistic field as a profession.
>
> —C.D.
>
> Dear C.D.: Dear Madam, just because he's not creative doesn't mean that he's not qualified in some other activity. Why don't you find out what he's interested in—or you may push him down the wrong path.

FB: Do you see Joyce often?

EB: We talk once a day or every other day—it's been even more since my husband died a few years ago. We visit all the time. We're friends. There's nothing I wouldn't do for her, not at any hour of the night, and she would do the same for me. And, as far as I know, we keep no secrets from each other.

FB: Did you push her to be a success?

EB: Never. She pushed herself. Joyce was bright from the start. She has a retentive mind—she has a way of closing herself off when she studies. At fifteen and a half, she went away to Cornell. But the courses weren't enough for her. She wrote home asking for more money so she could take more classes. Of course, we sent it to her.

FB: What did you think Joyce would want to be?

EB: Well, she was interested in the theater. She was a wonderful dancer—we thought she might pursue that. Then she went off into psychology.

FB: You and your husband were both lawyers. Did you want Joyce to be a lawyer too?

EB: Neither Morris nor I ever said, 'Come into the office.' I didn't do anything to push her. I was just there to help her when she needed it.

FB: There are a lot of parents who can't separate from their adult children.

EB: I don't have that problem. I don't even think of them as children—to me, they're friends.

> Dear Dr. Brothers' Mother:
>
> Whenever I spend a weekend with my daughter and her husband, I come away with the feeling that their marriage is about to fall apart. My daughter assures me, however, that they're very happy, though their arguments make me think the reverse is true. My husband and I rarely argued.
>
> —E.F.
>
> Dear E.F.: I would say mind your own business. Some husbands and wives enjoy these little tiffs. It adds a little spice —there's no rancor when it's finished. Just because you had one kind of marriage doesn't mean it's the only kind. The next day they go along the same way, as if it never happened. See, it's in your mind, not theirs.

FB: I'm sure you've seen parents who can't let go.

EB: Selfish, selfish, selfish. They kill the child. Nature provides that when a child is old enough, it feels its wings. If you don't let it, you're destroying the child's character.

FB: How are your daughters as mothers?

EB: They're the same as me. You learn to mother from your mother. Elaine always says, "I never force them to do anything. If I can't win the argument, I just stop. I cry alone."

FB: Do you cry alone too?

EB: I cry when I hear "The Star-Spangled Banner." I've had nothing else to cry about. My life has been very, very easy. My folks adored me. My husband made me feel important. The grandchildren call me. The great-grandchildren call me. . . .

> Dear Dr. Brothers' Mother:
>
> It makes me heartsick that neither of my daughters has married. I can't help but think this is all my fault, and often I can't sleep at night because I worry so about where I went wrong. My marriage to their father wasn't happy, but I tried to keep that from them. They're now both in their late thirties and tell me they have no intention of marrying. What can I do?
>
> —G.H.
>
> Dear G.H.: What do you want to do? Do you want to make them get married to please you? I think you want them to marry for your sake. You don't say, 'I want them to meet nice men and be happy.' You say, 'Where did I go wrong?' That's a declaration of self. There are a lot of women who haven't married and are very happy. Marriage is not the only fulfillment.

FB: What made you become a lawyer?

EB: I did it for my husband. I never had any great burning desire to be a lawyer. But he wanted the companionship, and I was happy to do it for him. We went to law school at the same time. And I was down at the office every day until he died.

FB: Were you partners?

EB: It was his practice. In the later years, before he died, he wanted to make me his partner. He had the papers drawn up;

he had the stationery printed. The children thought it was a wonderful idea. But I vetoed it. My ego didn't need it. I was happy to remain at his side, but I always felt that I wanted him to take the helm. I was happy to submerge my personality in his. Because we were very much in love.

Dear Dr. Brothers' Mother:

My husband is constantly complaining that he isn't successful because he doesn't make as much money as his father. But his father is a very unhappy man. He was a rotten father and a terrible husband. My husband loves our children and we have a wonderful marriage. I wish I could convince him that, to me, he is a great success.

—J.K.

Dear J.K.: Just keep repeating over and over how happy he is making you, what wonderful things he does. Just like a child wants some fairy stories read over and over again, your husband needs to hear over and over, "I am so very proud of you."

FB: Was your husband a very smart man?

EB: Very. Much, much smarter than me.

FB: Was it hard being together day and night?

EB: Not at all. We would come home at night, sometimes at nine or ten o'clock, and I would make a little dinner, and he would say, gratefully, "If I was married to anyone else, she'd never believe I'd been at the office so late."

FB: Did you help your daughters choose their mates?

EB: No. They both went to college, and they both met their respective husbands in college. Neither man was rich—it was just a question of affection. I remember when Joycie called me, and she was pinned.

Dear Dr. Brothers' Mother:

I have fallen deeply in love with a woman of a different faith. We've tried to break off our relationship because we realized the odds against us, but it didn't work. We love each other and we want to make this into a permanent, legal, long-term marriage. Both our families are bitterly opposed to the marriage, but, despite this, we feel we can't give each other up.

—L.M.

Dear L.M.: Well, right off the top of my head, I'd say if your affection is as great as you say it is, and you have the strength of character to make a good life, then I would go ahead. I would take a chance. I may be wrong. If you have the opportunity and lose it, you will always have it hanging over you.

FB: Were you concerned about the possibility of intermarriage in your family?

EB: No, we never had that problem. We were always connected with a temple. Our friends were Jewish—that's where we found our companions. But a lot of other people have had intermarriages, and it's worked out. It's a new world.

FB: What was your upbringing like?

EB: My parents were immigrants from Russia. My father was a soldier who ran away from the Russian army. He came here without anything at all. But within a year or two, he opened a dry goods store—and made a fortune. My mother, who came over with him, loved to work; she was always at the business. There were maids.

FB: Where did you grow up?

EB: In Williamsburgh, Brooklyn. Papa bought a big brownstone, and he brought over Mother's entire family. That's the kind of man he was. They all lived in the house: aunts, uncles, cousins. And there was always enough food. I've never wanted. I told you I wasn't very interesting. You wouldn't believe me.

Dear Dr. Brothers' Mother:

My husband's parents come from Poland and they have a great deal of prejudice towards blacks and Jews. Neither my husband nor I want to pass this on to our children, but we also don't want to hurt his parents' feelings. They are both in their eighties. How can we handle this?

—R.S.

Dear R.S.: I would avoid the subject. You can tell the children, 'That's not the way we feel,' but I would never try to change the parents. That's not your prerogative. You respect the grandparents by not arguing them down. You're not there to educate them. You love them for what they are. If they say something derogatory, you just let it go. I would close my eyes and ears to it. I would never, ever start a quarrel. You could make an enemy of the sweetest grandparents.

FB: You seem like a nice person.

EB: I don't fight. I get along. My mother had an expression: One argument brings another. One kiss brings another.

FB: How old were you when you met Morris Bauer?

EB: Fifteen. It was understood from the very start: nobody else. But I got married late. We just meandered along till the time came. It was a long courtship, but there was never any question of anyone else. And it worked: we were married for more than fifty years.

FB: It must have been hard to accept his death.

EB: Well, I felt that a great part of me left, because we had been together all the time. But I still talk about him. I refer to him quite a lot. I never shun conversation about him. It makes me feel like he's around and it makes life a little easier.

FB: That sounds like a very smart thing to do.

EB: No, I'm not smart. I've just lived a long time.

Dear Dr. Brothers' Mother:

Just recently my wife retired, and I find we're getting in each other's way. I really enjoyed having the house to myself, and while I love my wife and respect her, it seems a bit crowded now.

—T.W.

Dear T.W.: Are you doing anything? Have you got any projects? Did you prepare for retirement? You evidently didn't prepare at all. You really should seek something that interests you and pursue it. There's plenty of volunteer work—taking care of children, taking care of elderly people. You don't have to sit home and pretend you're having a good time when your days are really a blank.

FB: How is your retirement?

EB: Well, I have arthritis. And last winter I tripped on the sidewalk and fell face forward. I broke my right elbow. It's still very painful to move it.

FB: But you're cooking.

EB: I've got to do something. I keep busy. I'm very active. I visit my daughters, or they visit me. Elaine comes by all the time, and we go out to shows, we go out to dinner. Or I go to Joycie's farm. It's hard for me to remember that I'm more than fifty-five or sixty. Because I don't feel older. I do all the things I used to do.

FB: How old are you?

EB: Well over eighty.

FB: It sounds like you're very content.

EB: My family surrounds me—and all this warmth makes me think life is worth living. . . . I'm starting to feel like a Yiddishe mama talking to you.

FB: You've been lucky.

EB: When you go to nursing homes, and you hear the complaints—"my kid has forsaken me"—your heart bleeds. So I am very lucky.

FB: That's great.

EB: I told you I was boring. You didn't believe me.

Dear Dr. Brothers' Mother:

My father died in a nursing home after several years of not knowing who he or we, his family, were. It pains me to see my mother approaching her mid-eighties and realizing that the same fate may await her. She lives in a small apartment where she's relatively happy, but I can't help wondering about the future.

—Y.Z.

Dear Y.Z.: Why do you assume the same thing will happen to your mother? I think it's quite wrong, and your mother may even sense your attitude. You should support her, give her compliments. I don't think in terms of older people. It isn't age—it's the circumstances that go with it. If you're sick, you're sick. Some people are sick and old. And some old people carry on.

Abbie Hoffman's mother

FLORENCE HOFFMAN

"WE WERE ALWAYS WONDERING, 'WHAT NEXT?'"

"Yippie yes, yuppie no" is Abbie Hoffman's war cry. He was one of the most angry, dedicated, and, ultimately, effective radical leaders of the sixties. Twenty years later, Abbie is still fighting the system. Norman Mailer has called him "one of the bravest people I have ever met" and "a bona fide American revolutionary."

His outrageous acts are what people remember. In his heyday, Abbie dropped dollar bills onto the floor of the New York Stock Exchange (practically bringing trading to a standstill), he recruited a group of witches to levitate the Pentagon, and he plotted to spike the punchbowl at a White House lawn party with LSD.

But there was more than madness to his method. In 1968, at the height of his career as the great gadfly of his generation, Abbie Hoffman published a list of eighteen revolutionary demands. Most have long since been accomplished. The war in Vietnam—and the draft that powered it—are gone, as are (in many states) anti-abortion laws and harsh penalties for the use of marijuana. And environmental issues have become a major national concern. It's easy to forget that somebody had to start the ball rolling.

Abbie Hoffman would have kept the ball rolling if not for a 1973 cocaine bust. Facing a mandatory sentence of fifteen years to life, Hoffman went on the lam and, with a little help from his friends, managed to elude the FBI for nearly seven years. He emerged in 1980, did time, and then, unlike practically all his sixties cohorts, returned to a life of activism. These days Abbie is going after the nuclear power industry and rightist governments south of the border.

And what of Abbie's mother? During his years as a fugitive, Florence Hoffman sent him toothbrushes and dental floss via secret underground couriers, with notes reminding him that proper dental hygiene is important. And regardless of where he told her he was going, according to Abbie, Florence had the same response: "Dress warmly."

Recently, I met Abbie at Grossinger's, during a weekend marking the fifteenth anniversary of Woodstock (the rock festival took place a few miles from the famous Catskills resort). Over dinner of gefilte fish and flanken, we talked about nuclear war, Nicaragua, and the upcoming election. Then I asked Abbie to tell me more about his mother.

"I probably could've wiped out a McDonald's," he began, "and she would have said, 'My Abbie's a good boy. You don't know him like I do.' It's loyalty. It's nice, I guess—if you're her son.

"I just came back from Nicaragua. I called her from Miami. She said, 'Where are you?' I said, 'Miami. I just got back from Nicaragua.' She said, 'Nicaragua. That's nice. Aunt Rose is in the hospital. Her feet hurt.' I said, ' 'Bye, Ma. I'll call you soon.' I haven't called her.

"A lot happened in Nicaragua. I saw a people's revolution in progress, and I saw the U.S. Government trying to stop it. But that's not what we discussed. I've never had a political discussion with my mother in my life. It's not on her agenda. Except if I yell at Israel, she gets mad. She's gone off on a real Zionist kick.

"Actually, she might have supported what I was doing if she hadn't been intimidated by my father. They had a sort of old-fashioned relationship, so her views didn't prevail. In her era, women had their place. If she had a good idea or ambition, it was quickly dismissed as female frivolity.

"She even wanted to come to Chicago for the Chicago Seven trial, but my father wouldn't let her.

"Why did she give in? With her it's always been family first. She's a real traditional mother. I doubt that she ever voted differently from my father. I doubt that she even would have voted at all if he didn't take her.

"When I came aboveground, she came to New York and she said, 'My Abbie's a good boy.' She said it on TV, so she must have meant it.

"When I think of her, I think of the Merle Haggard song. You know, 'Mama Tried.' "

Several months before, I'd spent a day with Mama at her house in Worcester, Massachusetts. She tried. Florence Hoffman was nice enough to have me, but not confident enough to think that she had anything to say. So she spent the entire day in the kitchen. First she cleaned up from dinner the night before —she had had twelve relatives as guests. Then she served me an elaborate lunch consisting of roast beef and chicken and potatoes and cranberry sauce and chopped liver, and four kinds of dessert, and Shapiro's kosher wine. ("We really make a ceremony out of eating," said Florence. Then she added, "I mean I do. John's been gone ten years; I've got to start saying 'I.' ") And then she cleared the table, and then she washed the dishes. . . .

She was comfortable doing those things. She was distinctly uncomfortable talking about politics and Abbie. A typical exchange went like this:

"Do you approve of what Abbie accomplished in the sixties?"

"Have some chopped liver. . . ."

"Do you know what he accomplished?"

"Don't you like chopped liver?"

But the day was far from a total waste. We compromised. I ate the chopped liver, and occasionally Florence opened up.

"I can see now all the mistakes I made," she said at one point. "I don't think we really communicated. I don't think I communicate with him too well even now. There was nobody to give Abbott direction.

"And I don't think I praised him enough. My father was like that—nothing was ever good enough. He was raised that way.

To him I never accomplished anything. I tried to be better; maybe in the beginning I was like that, but I changed. I don't know if I changed too late."

At that point Florence showed me a school newspaper edited by her grandson, Hilario Ramos (the son of Abbie's sister, Phyllis, who is married to a Mexican government official). "I wrote him a letter telling him how great it is. So really I have changed."

Florence held up the newspaper proudly. "This," she told me, "is an example of what a child can do with proper guidance."

I first saw Florence Hoffman at the bus station in Worcester, where she'd come to pick me up. I had expected a younger woman—I'd forgotten that Abbie Hoffman is almost fifty. How old is his mother? "Seventy-eight," said Florence, whose accent makes her sound more like Rose Kennedy than anybody's Jewish mother. "Yeah, seventy-eight. I think."

With her was Abbie's first wife, Sheila. The mother of two of his three children, she married Abbie when he was still a radical-to-be. Summing up the conflict that led to their divorce six years later, Abbie said, "I'm reckless; she's cautious."

He could have been talking about his mother. Florence never went over twenty-five miles per hour as she drove us across town. She pointed out the sights—the temple where her husband was eulogized in 1974 ("I've never seen the place so crowded"), the high school from which Abbie was expelled. We were in a twenty-year-old Valiant. "No one touches this car but Florence Hoffman," said the driver. "It may sound selfish, but that's why it's lasted."

The house she takes us to is a white frame version of the Valiant. Little has changed in the forty-five years she's lived here—and little will change if she has her way. There are doilies to protect the end tables—from cut-glass bowls of candy and a relative's bar mitzvah picture—and antimacassars on the old sofa, and pads on the dining room table. It is a sober place. Scraps of lumber wait to be consumed in the fireplace, and no-frills cardboard boxes house Florence's cats ("Having a pet at this age brings a lot of life into your house," she tells me). The kittens are themselves wearing sensible collars. Nothing radical here.

But it was here that the King of the Yippies came of age. Says Florence, "Abbott is the older of the two. And from the start, he demanded a lot of attention. An awful lot. At three months, Abbott would get on his back and do acrobatics, for the whole family, like he was showing off."

When Jack, who now runs a restaurant in town, was born, Florence says, "Abbott was jealous. With my cats, they do the same thing. When I pet one, the other one gets jealous. But he got over it, I'm sure.

"Jack is such a doll, he really is," Florence goes on. "He was always surrounded by friends. It was a lively household. But Abbott was a difficult child to bring up. He had a few friends— not slews of them. He would bring home piles of books, up to here, and lock the door, to study. I don't think I took a great enough interest in what he was doing. I see that now.

"My daughter is much better, really much better as a mother," Florence says while casually setting the table. "She's interested in their homework and everything. I wish I had been. I'll take the blame, because I didn't have enough experience in raising children."

Perhaps she didn't have enough experience in raising Abbie Hoffman.

From the start, he was conscious of his status as a first-born Jewish son. In his memoirs, *Soon to Be a Major Motion Picture*, Abbie claims it is the burden of every first-born Jewish son to decide, early in life, whether to toe the line (by going to medical school, for instance) or "go for broke." Among the first-born Jewish sons who chose the more dangerous course, he says, were Marx, Einstein, and Freud.

And Hoffman. "By age thirteen," he says, "part of me had already begun to drop out of the mainstream." That year, the police came to the house looking for the person who was switching license plates on neighbors' cars. Florence suspected Abbie was guilty, but she shooed the cops away. A few years later, Florence was called into school. She remembers, "The teacher had said to Abbott, 'It's a wonder half of us aren't in the insane asylum because of you.' And Abbott piped up, 'What about the other half?' " He was eventually expelled for swinging at another teacher. But Florence says, "I wouldn't put all the blame on him. The whole class was disruptive."

Abbie's father, a druggist and a pillar of the local Jewish community, was less forgiving, and a battle raged between the two strongest-willed Hoffmans. Eventually, Abbie developed what he calls "one of the all-time great psychosomatic weapons" (and one his father's prescriptions couldn't cure): asthma. One doctor instructed Florence, "The patient should refrain from eggs, butter, milk, grains of all types, including bread, cereals, and pastries, poultry, and all sharp seasoning. Also he is to stay away from all animals with hair, feathers, ragweed, daisies, dandelions, and drafts. All dust should be removed from his room daily." Call it a prescription for a harassed mother.

There were also conflicts with her husband. "We were two different kinds of people. I'm a homebody," she says. "Johnnie was much more of a mixer. If it were up to me, he would have been home more." She also wanted to help out at work. She says, "I think I have a lot of business ability, but my husband didn't explain much to me, so I couldn't get involved."

Florence never rocked the boat. "Most men get their way," she says. "I went along, and things were placid. My whole life has always been my family."

For a while, it seemed like Abbie was on the right track. He found another high school, graduated with flying colors, and made his way to Brandeis University. Florence was impressed. "He had some fantastic professors," she says. "I went to visit, and I oohed and aahed. But I remember John was upset. He was such a neat person, about himself especially, and the kids at college didn't care about that stuff."

What were Florence's hopes for her first-born son? "John wanted him to get into medical school," Florence says. "I didn't outline any ambition for him at that time." But when Abbie told his parents he was studying to become a psychologist, "It hit me right," says Florence. "I thought, 'Psychology. Wow!' But I don't think it's the parents' decision. It's more the friends and teachers and the books you read than what you get at home."

Soon Abbie was more interested in civil rights and Vietnam than Psych. Says Florence, "I wasn't too well informed about politics. I know more now, but then, when I had to vote, I asked Johnnie who to vote for."

But she knew something was happening to Abbie, and she knew her husband didn't like it. Once Abbie's father told an interviewer, "He could have been somebody, a doctor or a professor. Now we have to read the papers to see which jail he's in." "He was always bemoaning that Abbie wasn't headed for a profession," Florence recalls, adding, "I think if he had had the right direction, he would have finished something stable."

"Isn't being a radical stable?" I ask Florence, now busy washing the dishes from lunch.

"I don't think you could call it stable," Florence answers. "We were always wondering, 'What next?' "

"But," she says, nonchalantly, while shutting off the water, "I guess Abbott enjoys it."

His parents obviously didn't. When Abbie spoke at Worcester's Holy Cross College (a speech he describes as "the return of a local boy made bad"), conservative alumni canceled five hundred thousand dollars in pledges. Abbie later wrote, "Me and the birth-control pill were just about the most celebrated things ever to come out of Worcester. At one time, most folks up there wished the pill had come first."

John lost valuable customers because of Abbie, and there was constant government surveillance of the house. "We were harassed a lot," says Florence. Once, while John was recuperating from a heart attack, Florence took him to Florida for a vacation. On the boardwalk, Florence was photographed by the same man she'd seen in Abbie's elevator in New York the day before. "I'm sure," she says, "that I'm in the FBI's files."

John died a few weeks after Abbie jumped bail on the coke charge. If the synagogue was full on the day he was buried, it may have been because platoons of government agents were there, hoping to nab the country's most-wanted radical as he said Kaddish.

I asked Florence about the period during which Abbie was
—to use her term—a "refugee." "It was scary," she says. "I
didn't see him enough."

But he did phone home, using a scrambling device so the
calls couldn't be traced. And he was able to see Florence four or
five times during his seven years in hiding. On one occasion, he
arranged for her to join him in Cuernavaca, Mexico. Says Florence, "I remember thinking, 'This one's looking at him too long;
that one's looking at him too long.' " Another time, Abbie arranged for Florence to be driven from Arizona to Los Angeles,
where they spent a day together at Disneyland, tempting the
fates. She remembers, "I was more scared than he was."

It is a period she obviously does not want to relive. "I have a
lot of clippings upstairs tied up with a piece of string," she says
matter-of-factly.

What about Abbie's books on the subject? "To tell you the
truth," she tells me truthfully, "I haven't finished *Soon to Be a
Major Motion Picture*. And the other one—something about
square dancing [*Square Dancing in the Ice Age*, which Abbie
dedicated to Florence]—I lent to my sister-in-law. So I'm just
starting it now."

I take one more shot: "How did you hold up while Abbie
was a fugitive?"

"I'm used to all kinds of adversity," she says while clearing
off the table. "Tell me, do you find life easy?"

Adversity first greeted Florence in Clinton, Massachusetts,
where her mother labored in a sweatshop and her father was a
wrecker. Her ambition was to be a physical therapist, but she
settled for a job as payroll clerk at a woolen factory. When the
company transferred her to New York, she recalls, "I lived in
the Y, where there were a lot of revolutionary speakers. But I
wasn't interested." She also hated the "fast pace" of New York
and quickly returned to her job in Worcester. There she met her
future husband, bowling.

Before she married John Hoffman, Florence traveled as a
competitive gymnast. After one meet, in Buffalo, she was with a
group of German students in a bar. "They started saying, 'Heil,
Hitler,' " Florence recounts. "I didn't know what to do. I didn't

know if I should quit the team or not. So I just left. I'm sure Abbie would have spoken up."

Her tone betrays a grudging admiration, so I press her. (After all, my time is almost up—the table is completely cleared.) "Do you respect Abbie for what he did?"

"I think my husband was not for it, really," she says. BUT WHAT DID YOU THINK? "I was scared for him," says Florence. (I notice she is finally saying "I" instead of "we.") "But Abbott was always very bright. He foresaw all these wrongs in the world."

Florence goes on: "There are times when you think, 'Gosh, he was right for speaking up.' My husband probably thought so inwardly, but he never expressed it."

Says Florence, "Abbott leaves a lesson: Be aware of what's happening around you. I think that's a good lesson."

It is a lesson Abbie Hoffman's mother is taking to heart. She has recently joined two public affairs discussion groups at which, for the first time in her life, she is expressing her political opinions.

Maybe life begins at eighty.

Neil Sedaka's mother

ELEANOR SEDAKA

"WHEN HE'S ON TV, I HAVE TO WATCH HIM ALL
ALONE, SO I CAN SCREAM AND CRY WITHOUT ANY-
BODY THINKING I'M CRAZY."

*I was in the Lake Tarleton Hotel, and some women realized who
I was. They followed me into the powder room, and they said,
"Your son is so wonderful. The way he sings, the way he plays
the piano—certainly you must have a talent, too." And I said,
"Sure, I have a talent. I'm his mother."*

It's a talent Eleanor Sedaka almost didn't get to show off. In
1938, a year and a half before Neil was born, Eleanor gave birth
to a daughter, Ronnie. So difficult was the pregnancy that the
doctor had warned her, "No more children."

As Neil wrote in his memoirs, *Laughter in the Rain*, "Eleanor Sedaka tried every roller coaster in Coney Island in their
order of ferocity: the Tornado, the Bobsled, the Virginia Reel,
the Thunderbolt, and the monstrous Cyclone. She was three
months pregnant and was trying to abort the child—me."

*He's such a marvelous person. He has such a fine character. He's
good. He's like a piece of fresh rye bread.*

Judging from her comments forty-five years later, Eleanor
Sedaka is glad Neil survived Coney Island. But ironically, her
visit there foreshadowed his career, which by his own admission

has been "like riding the monstrous Cyclone." From the choral group at Abraham Lincoln High School, Neil Sedaka emerged as a teenage superstar with hits like "Oh, Carol" (a tribute to then-steady girlfriend Carole King), "Stupid Cupid," and "Stairway to Heaven." He was a millionaire in short order, and on his concert tours, Eleanor says, "he had to climb out bathroom windows, or they would have killed him."

Then, in 1963, with the arrival of the Beatles, Neil's career careened off the tracks. For nearly a decade, he toiled in semi-obscurity, gained weight, and worried about how he would support his family.

But in 1975, with the hit "Laughter in the Rain," Neil began a comeback that, his mother brags, "was bigger than Sinatra's."

Some days, I'll be playing Mah-Jongg, and the radio is on. And I'll hear Neil singing, and it's like he's singing to me. And on the outside, I'll stay calm, but inside, everything is jumping.

Eleanor Sedaka greets me at the door of her house in Fort Lauderdale. The place is spotless; even her garage is carpeted. Eleanor herself is blond, impeccably coiffed, and wearing a perfectly tailored pantsuit. Her jewelry includes a bracelet made of gold-and-diamond *E*'s, a gift, she says, from Neil. "He is so generous. He always calls and says, 'Mother, what do you want?' I say, 'Nothing.' And he says, 'Come on, there must be something.' "

This is the dream house Eleanor shared with her husband of forty-six years, Mac Sedaka, until he died in 1982. "Everything was perfect," she says, "until the big C came and ruined our lives. Mostly his." Eleanor still gets teary-eyed when speaking of her husband, whom she called Dad. "Why God had to take him I don't know," she says. "There are so many bastards.

"You can get used to everything—even the bad," Eleanor observes. Then, she says, "Sometimes, I'll be sitting outside, and a bird will fly down, and it watches me, and watches me, and I say to myself, 'That's Dad.' I know he's with me, and I feel secure."

Her role as a wife has been taken from her, but Eleanor is still a mother.

I'll be in a store, and they'll see my credit card, and they'll say, "Are you related to . . ." And I'll say, "What, darling?" And they'll say, "Are you related to Neil Sedaka?" And I'll say, "In a way. I'm his mother."

The musical talent came from Eleanor's side of the family. Her mother and father met performing in a silent movie house in the Bronx. She played the piano; he the drums. Eleanor's father also wrote songs. She remembers one, "Let a Smile Be Your Umbrella."

But Eleanor remembers little of her parents. Orphaned at four, she was raised by a grandmother who "gave me more love than I would have had from ten mothers." Her grandmother was poor, and Eleanor had cousins who were wealthy. "They wanted to adopt me. My grandmother tried to take me there, figuring it would be a better life. But I absolutely refused to leave, and I was right. Thanks to my grandmother, I knew how to be a good mother."

At fourteen, Eleanor went to work as a milliner; she remembers, "the boss would give us a few hours off a week to go to 'continuation school.' " At seventeen, she met Menahem Sedacca (she later changed the spelling of his name), and the pressure from family and friends to marry him was intense. Eleanor didn't love Mac then, but she consented—it was important to have a provider.

Mac drove a taxi. In those days he made eleven dollars a week. The two-bedroom apartment in Brooklyn into which Ronnie and Neil were born was home to nine Sedaccas, and to the lusty cooking odors provided by Mac's Sephardic relatives, who spoke not Yiddish but Ladino.

Eleanor wore the pants in the family. "My husband was a dear, sweet man who, when he lay down at night, didn't want headaches. He let me rule the roost." But Mac also doted on his wife, whom he called "Skinny" because she weighed eighty-four pounds at the altar.

"He treated me like I was made of glass. If something dropped," she remembers, "he wouldn't let me bend over to pick it up."

Eleanor, however, was far from idle. Neil remembers, "My mother never let me do anything for myself. She even fed me till I was seven." Eleanor admits that, explaining, "He was a very poor eater."

Before long, he was taking his meals at the piano. As Eleanor remembers it, "When Neil was seven, the school called. I went down there. And they said, 'Do you know, your son conducts the orchestra like a professional.' I said, 'That's nice.' And they said, 'What do you intend to do about it? Are you going to buy him a piano?' I told them we couldn't afford one, but they convinced me." So Eleanor went to work as a department store cashier, and later as a bra model, to earn money for a piano.

Neil and Ronnie both took lessons. "The first teacher," Eleanor recalls, "said, 'She's good. He's not.' So we got rid of that one." Soon Neil was taking lessons on Saturdays at Juilliard and, Eleanor recalls, "music was his whole life. You couldn't make him a doctor or a lawyer."

It was her dream to make him a concert pianist. And so, when Neil asked her if he could switch into pop music, Eleanor was devastated. "I finally told him he could take six months off if he would make three promises: You don't leave my house till you get married, you marry someone of your own faith, and you stay away from dope." Says Eleanor, "He made, and kept, all three."

Still, there were problems. At sixteen, Neil began receiving royalty checks that dwarfed his parents' income. According to Eleanor, "Neil said, 'I want you to redo the apartment so gorgeous that people will drop dead when they walk in the door.' And I did." But she wouldn't let *him* spend his money. "He wanted a Cadillac, and he could have afforded it, but I made him buy a Chevy. I said, 'You don't start from the top.' "

Eleanor controlled the purse strings while Neil was dating Carole King ("she used to drive me up the wall; she was always coming around") and later when he was courting Leba Strassberg, whose mother, Esther, owned the famous Catskills resort Esther Manor.

Neil married Leba when he was twenty-two. Remembers Eleanor, "The wedding was in September, and Dara was born in June. Everyone was counting on their fingers, but it wasn't true."

Soon after his marriage, Eleanor announced that she was raising Neil's allowance to $225 a week. Not surprisingly, Leba and Eleanor clashed over that arrangement. But it wasn't until 1966, when Neil was twenty-seven, that he finally demanded control of his money.

In his book, Neil remembers that when he broke the news to his mother, she became hysterical. Later he learned she had taken an overdose of sleeping pills and had to be rushed to the hospital.

When he's on TV, I have to watch him all alone, so I can scream and cry without anybody thinking I'm crazy.

Ten years ago, around the time Neil was beginning his comeback, Eleanor and Mac retired to Fort Lauderdale, when "you couldn't buy a menorah here and people didn't know what matzoh meal was." But they knew Neil Sedaka. "He would come down," Eleanor recalls, "and play shuffleboard with the men. And he'd bowl on his father's team, and he'd ride his bicycle and wave."

My friends call me and say, "Neil's on TV tomorrow." But I never call them, even if I know first. If someone says, "Why didn't you tell me?" I say, "I just found out myself." I let the others do the talking. But I wouldn't say I don't enjoy it.

Eleanor is still adjusting to her husband's death. She spends her time with other widows, playing Mah-Jongg, canasta, and poker, and going out to dinner. She says, "I don't go out with couples anymore. It doesn't feel right."

*It seems like every time there's a workman in the house, he says,
"Do you happen to have an autographed picture of Neil?" And
I say, "I'm not sure, dear; let me see." And then I say, "Well,
you're in luck. I do."*

When she can, Eleanor visits Ronnie, who's married to a
chemist in Las Vegas ("but in Vegas, you can't even find four
Jews for Mah-Jongg") or Neil, who lives in Connecticut with
Leba and their two children. "I'm a typical Jewish mother," she
says. "My children were, are, and always will be my life."

No doubt she'd like to forget the Cyclone.

*Long after he's gone, my son will be remembered. How many
mothers can say that?*

Rosalyn Yalow's mother

CLARA SUSSMAN

"HER TEACHER SAID, 'YOUR DAUGHTER IS A GENIUS.'
AND I THOUGHT, 'GENIUS? I DON'T WANT A
GENIUS. I WANT A NORMAL CHILD.' "

Clara Sussman is the oldest person I have ever met.

"I'm ninety-nine and one month and six days," she tells me proudly.

She was five in 1890, when her family traveled by ferry from Hamburg, Germany, to Liverpool, and then by steamship from Liverpool to New York. She remembers the journey distinctly.

In her later years, Clara saw the Wright Brothers fly, and she remembers the excitement caused by the sinking of the *Maine* in Havana in 1898. Once, she watched the President make a speech from the back of a train. The President was William McKinley.

"I can't tell you how many times I've wanted to write a book about my life," she tells me.

Certainly, the mind is willing. "I think I have a little sense left," Clara jokes. She still devours books and newspapers— "Anything you bring, I'll read."

But the flesh may be a little weak. Two months before I interviewed her, Clara had suffered a disabling stroke. That's when she moved from her home in Rockaway, Queens to a nursing home in the Bronx. (Kid sister Sue Zipper, ninety-three, her housemate in Rockaway, moved with her.) She receives daily therapy. "They're teaching me to walk," says Clara.

"Until two months ago," she says, "I was a healthy woman going around minding my own business. I like to keep busy. I've left my furniture in Rockaway. And I'm still paying rent. I'm going back there.

"I try to keep my spirits up," adds Clara. "The trouble is, I was spoiled. I've really and truly had a good life.

"So I'm feeling a little let down by the stroke," she says. "Sometimes, I look at this wheelchair, and I get angry at myself. I say, 'What are you sitting in that chair for, Clara?'

"It hit so fast."

Then she says, emotionally, "I asked Ros to see what she could do about curing strokes."

The answer is: maybe a lot. Clara's daughter Ros is Rosalyn Yalow, who seven years ago became the second woman in history to win a Nobel Prize for medicine. Rosalyn's award recognized her role in developing radioimmunoassay, a laboratory procedure that employs radioisotopes to measure with a high degree of precision substances in the blood or other body fluids. Used in tens of thousands of laboratories around the world to detect everything from diabetes to drug addiction, it is considered one of the greatest advances in clinical medicine since World War II. The Nobel Prize was only one in a long series of honors Yalow has accumulated in her forty years of research, most of them at the VA Hospital in the Bronx, where she puts in eighty-hour workweeks.

Rosalyn invited Clara to the Nobel ceremony in Stockholm. "She wanted me to go in the worst way," says Clara. "But I was ninety-two, and it was wintertime. I didn't want to spoil her fun."

Instead, Clara enjoyed the honor from afar. "I was at my doctor's, and he said to everyone, 'This is the Nobel Prize winner's mother,' and they all applauded.

"The *Times*," Clara adds proudly, "called her 'The Madame Curie from the Bronx.' "

Which makes Clara the Madame Curie's mother from Wellsville, Ohio.

It was in that town, then home to fewer than two thousand people, that Clara Zipper came of age. She remembers, "There was no prejudice against Jews there—I don't think they even knew what a Jew was. My father had to go to Cleveland, a hundred miles away, to go to shul. And every year, my mother had to send away for matzohs. But we were very Reform—you know, the German Jews were a little different from the Russians."

They also had more money. "There were a lot of doctors and lawyers in my mother's family," Clara says. Her father was a "high-class" tailor in Berlin (he'd learned his trade during more than a decade in the army) with many men in his employ. But one by one, they left to go to the United States. "One week, my father lost seven workers," Clara says. "So he said, 'They're all going to America. We're going to America too.' My mother was heartbroken. But it was the smartest thing he ever did in his whole life. Because later we lost a lot of family in the war."

The Zippers lived in New York, then in Philadelphia. They pulled up roots again when a job became available in Wellsville. "It was a country town—we had our own chickens," says Clara. "We were brought up very nice.

"But Mama wanted us to marry Jews," says Clara, who had five brothers and sisters. So the Zippers moved back to New York when Clara was thirteen. Their first home was in the Yorkville section of Manhattan. Then they moved to what Clara remembers as a pretty suburb with red brick houses: Harlem.

Clara had finished the sixth grade in Wellsville. An average student, she remembers, "I was never stupid—that I know—but I don't think I was ever smart." In New York, she didn't bother going to school. Instead, at thirteen, she took her first job —as a salesgirl at Blumstein's, a department store on 125th Street, for three dollars a week.

College was not an option. "Girls didn't go to college then," she says. "It was hard enough for Jewish boys to get into college." But she could have gone to high school—in fact, she says, her parents encouraged her to do so. So why didn't she? Says Clara, "I thought I was so grown up, so independent."

Still, after a taste of independence, Clara vowed that if she married and had children, "they would go to college—to make something of themselves." She did marry, after meeting Simon Sussman at a dance ("At one time, I could dance") and discovering that, "to me, he was the best man in the world." And she did have children: first Alexander, then, two years later, Rosalyn.

"I carried her for ten months," Clara claims. "On the night she was born, she was looking all around already. The doctor said, 'This one is gonna be a smart one.' "

When Rosalyn was two, Clara says, "If I read her a story, and I changed one word from the night before, she knew. I don't know if she memorized or if she read."

She was also strong-minded. When her brother was recuperating from an operation, Rosalyn, wearing a homemade nurse's uniform, took over. Says Clara, "If he needed a pill, I couldn't give it to him. I had to give it to her to give to him."

While attending grade school in the Bronx, Rosalyn "always used to come home with gold stars," says Clara. At ten, she started junior high school, which meant traveling across the Bronx by trolley. The first day, Clara followed her onto the trolley; she planned to watch from the next car. But when Rosalyn spotted Clara, she got off and waited for another trolley. That night, Clara recalls, Rosalyn said, "Don't follow me. My friends will think I'm a baby."

Clara never followed her again. "She was independent; she had a strong mind of her own. But I never stopped her, because I was independent myself."

Rosalyn entered Hunter College at fifteen. According to Clara, "Once her teacher called me in and said, 'You know, your daughter is a genius.' And I thought, 'Genius? I don't want a genius. I want a normal child.' I was thinking of Albert Einstein. I never met the man, but I had heard he was a little peculiar."

But there was no stopping Rosalyn. At twenty, she left for graduate school at Illinois (where she became the second woman ever to earn a Ph.D. in physics). "My husband wanted to pay her fare," says Clara. "She said, 'I'll pay my own way and I'll pack my own valise. I don't want my parents to stand on the platform and say, "Our baby's going away." ' " Adds Clara, "She was so independent, but she was nice about it. I let her do what she wanted—as long as I thought it was right."

Rosalyn returned the favor. Toward the end of World War II, when everyone was working, Clara wanted to get a job. She was sixty.

"I told my husband, 'I'm going to work,' and he said, 'Over my dead body.' He told me, 'People will say I can't support you.' [Simon, who died in 1959, had a small paper and twine business.] But I had nothing to do at home but worry—my son was in the army. So Ros wrote a letter to my husband. It said, 'It's war; if she can work, she should.' So I went to work looking over the orders in a shirt house." Simon wanted her to quit her job when the war ended. But by then, observes Clara, "I had him trained."

When she was sixty-five, Clara fell on the steps of a subway station and then she had to quit her job. Says Clara, "I loved to work. I loved going downtown and mixing with all the people. If I didn't break my leg, I'd still be working."

Clara became a volunteer, helping retarded children and raising money for an organization for the blind in Israel. She spent time with her son, a retired civil servant who died in 1980 ("to lose a son isn't an easy thing"). And she spent time with Rosalyn, her husband, Aaron, and their two children, Benjamin and Elanna—indeed, she came to the house every day until both children were in school.

These days, it's Rosalyn who does the visiting. "She comes all the time," says Clara. "She's such a busy person, how she finds the time, I don't know. And when she doesn't come, her husband comes. Believe me, she married the right man. He did a lot of things for her. If he wasn't such a good person, she couldn't have gotten as far as she did."

Then, too, Rosalyn did a lot for Aaron, a physics professor at the Cooper Union. "He's a rabbi's son," says Clara, "and Ros promised she would keep a kosher home. They used to come to my house with their own food and paper plates. She's married forty-two years, and she still does it. Not many girls would bother.

"This is the kind of person she is."

Rosalyn made her mother proud when she accepted an invitation to speak in the Soviet Union—then drew attention to the plight of Soviet Jews by meeting with Refuseniks. "I would have taken a stand myself," says Clara. "I'm proud to be a Jew. I was never religious. But I went to a Reform temple every Saturday, and I took the children. I tried to do the best I can."

According to Clara, Rosalyn has never put on airs. "She's a very ordinary person. If she wasn't, I wouldn't like her so much." Still, Clara would like to see her daughter pamper herself a little more (for years, Clara nagged Rosalyn to buy a mink coat) and she'd also like her to slow down. "She works so hard; she travels so much. I think she's overdoing it. She's no chicken anymore. But she says, 'What am I going to do? Stay home and mop the floor?' "

It isn't likely. Rosalyn will keep right on fighting for human life. And her mother will keep right on learning to walk.

A few months after my meeting with Clara, I received the following message from Rosalyn:

"My mother passed away on July 8 [1985], just 8 days short of her 100th birthday. She was admitted to Montefiore [Hospital] in early May for a diverticulitis. On her return to Beth Abraham [nursing home] she never fully regained her strength. I was with her at the Montefiore Emergency Room when the end came. I know she would have liked to see the book."

❦ Robert Klein's ❦
mother

FRIEDA KLEIN

"I SAID TO THE DRESSMAKER, 'I'M ROBERT KLEIN'S
MOTHER,' AND SHE SAID, 'THAT'S NICE. I LIKE
BUDDY HACKETT.'"

I first met Frieda Klein in an auditorium at New York University. I had come to see *The Robert Klein Show*—a two-hour concert that would later become an HBO special. Before the lights went down, I introduced myself to Rory Rosegarten, the comedian's associate producer, who told me Robert's mother had flown up from Florida to see the show.

Once I knew that, it wasn't hard to find her. Sitting among the hundreds of college students in the auditorium was one Rosalind Russell lookalike in a white pantsuit. I went over, introduced myself, and sat down next to her. For the next two hours, Frieda Klein was my interpreter and tour guide. She introduced me to her husband, Ben (who died a few months later, after fifty-two years of marriage), and a succession of cousins, step-cousins, and cousins-in-law who had come to see the show. And she told me about Robert's career: how he trained with Chicago's Second City comedy troupe (the alma mater of Gilda Radner, Dan Aykroyd, and John Belushi), how he was discovered by Rodney Dangerfield at the Improvisation in Manhattan, how he was given his start on television by Johnny Carson, how he has appeared on every major talk show, how he performs all over the world, and how he won a Tony nomination for

They're Playing Our Song, the Broadway musical in which he starred for fourteen months.

When the show began, I quickly realized that Frieda is Robert's biggest fan. "That's funny," she would say after a punch line. "That's really funny." If I laughed, she seemed happy; if I didn't, she explained the joke to me. And then, when it was all over, Frieda—and I—led a standing ovation.

The next day, it is Frieda's turn to perform—for me. The setting is Robert's apartment, a sprawling Fifth Avenue duplex. But the comedian is still asleep, and his wife, Brenda Boozer, the opera star, is on the road, along with their toddler son, Alexander. It is Ben who greets me at the door. For a few minutes we chat. Robert, in his official bio, describes Ben as "a good living room comedian," and it's true, he is. But Ben knows I've come to interview his wife. "I'll leave you now," he says to Frieda. "Don't tell no bad stories."

"I'll only tell the good parts," Frieda promises.

Luckily, there are lots of good parts. Frieda's life has taken her from the Upper East Side of Manhattan, where she met her childhood sweetheart, to the Bronx and Queens, where she married him and raised two "marvelous" children, to a Florida retirement community, where she found a new career at seventy-one. Five years ago, Frieda's friends talked her into playing the piano at a Hadassah luncheon—it was her first time performing in public. Frieda was a smash, and now she is booked at one charity affair after another. She also has a regular gig, accompanying fashion shows put on by a local dress shop. "I don't do it for money," she says. "Just for fun."

Naturally, I ask Frieda to play for me. She sits down at her daughter-in-law's Steinway, and suddenly the room is filled with music. Gershwin. Cole Porter. "Does it sound like I can't read a note?" she asks me. "No? That's what they tell me. I didn't want to practice, so my mother stopped the lessons."

I ask her if she has any desire to take lessons now. "I can fake it so well; why should I? Robert wants me to go back and study. But I don't think I need it."

Frieda is racing through more Porter, and for an added

touch of class, she plays with one hand crossed over the other. "Do you know why I did that?" she asks. "Because I saw a real pianist do it.

"To me, playing is just like breathing," Frieda goes on. "I do it when I'm happy; I do it when I'm sad. But I never thought I'd play for three hundred and fifty Hadassah women. That was really something."

She is starting another song. It is her own composition: " 'Rhapsody in Red,' I call it." Then she plays "Tea for Two," then "Small Hotel"—"my favorite song." That reminds her to play "My Favorite Things." Then she plays "Someone to Watch over Me." "This is a Gershwin tune," she says. "My own arrangement."

When she's done, I give her a standing ovation. Robert isn't there, but I know that if he were, he'd be applauding just as hard as Frieda did last night.

"He's a wonderful comedian," she says. "And he thinks I'm the best piano player."

For two hours, Frieda and I talked, and I recorded her thoughts.

On Robert's success:

" *Thank God he made it. There's plenty of good talent that will never be heard from. When he said he wanted to be an actor, I thought, 'We'll have to support him for the rest of his life.' *"

On doing housework:

" *Housework is a drag—I'll be very honest. I think it's a thankless job. But you have to do it, whether you like it or not.*

" *When Robert was nine and Rhoda was thirteen, I went to work at Montefiore Hospital in the Bronx. I did it as a joke. I said to the family, 'There I'll be appreciated.' And I was. I loved it. I felt important. At first they only needed someone for a month. But I ended up staying for fifteen years, as a medical secretary.*

" *Benny didn't want me to work. He said, 'I make a good salary.' His ego was hurt. Now I think the way your generation thinks, but then I didn't. I'm sorry that I didn't go farther with my career.*"

On being sad or angry:

" *When I feel sad or angry, I take out a piece of paper and I write down in shorthand my truest thoughts—everything— in the vilest language. Then I throw it away so it hurts no one.*"

On getting old:

" *I can't lie about my age anymore, because I just had a seventy-fifth birthday party. But I don't mind. I hope someday to be able to say I'm ninety. [She starts to cry.] Two years ago, I had a mastectomy. I'm not crying because I want sympathy. I'm crying because I'm just so glad to be here.*

" *The American Cancer Society wanted me to go around to hospitals to cheer people up. But I can't. I can take care of myself, but with anybody else I'd fall apart.*"

On Robert's marriage:

" *They lived together for sixteen months. Thank God they got married.*

" *I told him, 'Your wife comes before your parents. You compliment her, admire her, and hug and kiss her.' And I meant it. I think Robert and Brenda are ideally mated. They're good for each other, they really are.*

" *Did I mind that it was an intermarriage? Not really. I respect every religion. Brenda comes from a beautiful family. They're all doctors—I made a joke that they could own a hospital. They laughed—but it turns out they do.*

" All except Brenda's father—he's a Methodist minister. He just came back from Israel. He knows more about the Jewish religion than we do."

On Robert's wedding:

" They had a beautiful wedding in Atlanta, Georgia. They had all the Jewish foods for us—like Tam-Tam crackers with chopped liver. Of course, they also had roast beef sandwiches with mayonnaise. That's a no-no."

On coming to visit Robert:

" They give me things to do, errands, to make it easier for them, which I enjoy. They're so busy, you can't imagine. Naturally, their careers come first.

" But I can't shop at the expensive markets on Madison Avenue. When I look at the prices there, I get sick. So I go over to Third Avenue, and I walk back with the shopping bags.

" I grew up in hard times. No matter how much money Robert has, I don't think I'll change."

On being the mother of a celebrity:

" Sometimes I take advantage of being Robert's mother. My husband doesn't like to, but I do. Like we went to see a show at the Sunrise Theater, in Fort Lauderdale, and there was a long line outside. So I went to the door where they let the entertainers in, and I said who we are, and we went right in. Sometimes, it pays. But once, I went to the dressmaker and I said, 'I'm Robert Klein's mother,' and she said, 'That's nice. I like Buddy Hackett.' I never went back to her."

On meeting famous people:

" When Robert opened in They're Playing Our Song, we went to Sardi's. Neil Simon was there. And then I met Lucille Ball

Leah Adler with son Steven Spielberg
outside her Beverly Hills dairy restaurant.

Leah Greenburg
with son Dan
Greenburg today
and during his
undergraduate
years at the
University of
Illinois.

Naomi Birnbach
with daughter
Lisa Birnbach
in 1976.

Kate Stupp
with son
Eddie Fisher.

Francine Rich with husband Rob and sons Adam (foreground) and Wayne in their backyard.

Eleanor Sedaka with son Neil Sedaka today and with his sister Ronnie in Brooklyn in the fifties.

Clara Sussman with daughter Rosalyn Yalow and granddaughter Elanna.

Frieda Klein with husband Ben and
son Robert Klein in Jerusalem.

Frieda with daughter
Rhoda at Robert's
graduation from
Alfred University.

Sylvia Wallace with husband Irving, son David Wallechinsky and daughter Amy.

Gerry Dreyfuss with son Richard Dreyfuss.

Linda Gaylord with son Mitch Gaylord just after the Olympics.

Linda with husband Fred and sons Mitch (left) and Chuck.

Fraydele Oysher
with daughter
Marilyn Michaels
in 1958 and 1980.

Clara Smirnoff and son Yakov
on the set of _Brewster's Millions._

Clara and Yakov
in Odessa.

Ron Galella

Jackie Fierstein celebrating son Harvey Fierstein's thirtieth birthday in 1984.

Florence with son
Gene Simmons
backstage at a Kiss
concert and at home
in Israel in
the forties.

Razie Streicher with son
Harry Reems in 1980.

Harry's high school
graduation picture.

Ruth Manchester with daughter Melissa
Manchester in Los Angeles.

Ruth with
daughters
Claudia (left)
and Melissa
in New York
in 1960.

Marilyn Bernstein with husband
Milton, daughter Elizabeth, and son
Fred in New York in 1963.

—her daughter was in the show. It was so exciting. Robert is friends with Rodney Dangerfield—he has two very nice children. Of course, Marvin Hamlisch was here for the bris. They had a lot of people here, and all the nice Jewish food. I wanted to play a duet with Marvin, but he had to leave, with Cyndy Garvey. He's going out with her, you know.

" *I love meeting them. Robert says he's in the right profession for his mother.*"

On meeting Mary Tyler Moore—almost:

" *Once, Robert took us to Israel, and you know who he met there? Mary Tyler Moore, one of my favorite actresses. She was there with Dr. Levine. We were walking in Jerusalem, and I heard someone say, 'Oh, hello, Robert. What are you doing here?' But I didn't see who it was. Robert says he called to me, but I didn't hear him. I told him, 'I'll never forgive you.'* "

On meeting Benny:

" *We grew up together—my sister and his sister were friends. But I didn't like him. He was a nasty kid.*

" *I got to know him better when my father died. His mother came to pay a shivah call; I can still see her walking down the street with two big chickens. Then I started going with Benny and his family to Coney Island.*"

On courting Benny:

" *Eventually, we started dating. But in those days, you didn't live together till you got married. Once, when I was sixteen, he took me in the bedroom and he kissed me. His mother was banging on the door, yelling, 'Leave that girl alone.'* "

On their big night out:

" *He worked for two months after school, for a florist, a butcher, and a baker, to earn the money to take me to a movie on Broadway—it was* The Big Parade, *with Victor McLaglen —and a pastry shop on Southern Boulevard, where all the young folks went. And he wanted to take a cab. But nice girls weren't supposed to take a cab. I don't know why; I guess the guy might try to kiss you.*

" *He wouldn't marry me till he was making a good living. He couldn't see living with our parents. So he went to work as a textile salesman. But it was understood that we would marry. I think maybe, when we weren't seeing each other for a month, I went out with one other guy. My sister got me a date, which was a disaster.*"

Benny (who has just walked into the room): "Now you tell me?"

On getting married:

" *We finally got married when I was twenty-three. My mother said to him, 'Which is it, yes or no?' It was a shotgun wedding.*"

On their life together:

" *We've stayed together fifty-two years; it couldn't be that bad. But I don't want you to think everything was always hunkydory. Not that he ever went out with other women. But marriage is a compromise. You can't do everything on your own. You have to consult the other person.*"

On what she wanted her son to be:

" *Whatever he wanted to be.*"

On what he wanted to be:

" At first, a doctor. Whenever we had a pain, he'd want to know about it. When he was twelve, he'd bring home books about anatomy.

" Then he discovered acting. I wasn't too happy, because not too many people make it. They wait for their ships to come in. But he worked, he did odd jobs, he didn't ask for anything.

" When he was at Alfred University, he was vice-president of the Footlight Club. We went up and spoke to his two drama coaches. They told us Robert was the best talent to come along in nineteen years."

On whether Robert was funny as a child:

" You know, I don't remember. Benny, was Robert funny?"

Benny: "Nah, he was an average kid. He played baseball."

On her daughter, Rhoda Cohen, an elementary school teacher:

" Here, let me show you a picture." [She reaches into her bag.]

Benny: "She's got hammers and bricks in there. You couldn't lift that thing."

" Here. This was taken last summer, in Westhampton. She's really a nice person. They're both such good children."

On why they're such good children:

" Because we're such good parents."

On her looks:

" People used to say, 'You're so beautiful.' Now they tell me I'm a 'handsome' woman."

On moving to Florida:

" *I didn't want to go. But Benny said, 'Either come with me, or we'll correspond.' I'm a poor corresponder, so I went.*

" *Florida's a little boring. It was much nicer when we first moved down there, when everyone was younger. The biggest excitement this year was when we had an alligator in the canal by our house. We fed it bagels. They say if it's more than six feet long, you have to call the police. Now I want to know: Who's going to measure it?"*

David Wallechinsky's mother

SYLVIA WALLACE

"I CHECKED WITH MY CHILDREN, AND THEY DO LOVE ME."

Sylvia Wallace would be right at home in a book about successful women: a magazine editor at eighteen, she went on to write two best-selling novels and collaborate on several nonfiction best-sellers. And she would be an ideal subject for a book on wives of famous men: her husband, Irving Wallace, has authored thirty-two books—fifteen of them novels—which together have sold an incredible 200 million copies.

So what's she doing in *this* book? Sylvia's daughter and son, Amy Wallace and David Wallechinsky, are themselves best-selling authors. Amy started out by producing *The Two* (about the original Siamese twins). Her brother began his career with a book on organic gardening and *What Really Happened to the Class of '65?*, about his high school cohorts. Then Amy, David, and their father wrote *The Book of Lists* and *The People's Almanac*, both blockbusters. Finally, Sylvia got into the act, co-writing, with her son, daughter, and husband, *The Book of Lists 2* and *The Intimate Sex Lives of Famous People*. As *People* magazine proclaimed, in an article on the Wallaces' unprecedented yours-mine-and-ours literary endeavors, "The family that writes together soars to publishing heights together."

Amy Wallace does her soaring in Berkeley. David lives and works in Santa Monica. Irving and Sylvia are based in Brentwood, the ritzy section of West L.A., in a seventeen-room combined home and office. There, I was greeted by one of the Wallaces' secretaries, who assured me I had chosen a worthy subject for my book: "Mrs. Wallace is a terrific mother." A few minutes later, I met Mrs. Wallace, who was equally quick to assure me that the secretary was only being kind: "She hasn't worked here long enough to know."

Sylvia, a blond wisp of a woman, led me into Irving's office —a giant (forty-foot by fifty-foot) study that connects the residential and office wings of the house. Why, with seventeen rooms to choose from, did Sylvia decide to see me in her husband's office, I began to wonder. But the answer presented itself when Irving walked into the room—and the affection between husband and wife became apparent. Cheery-faced and puffing on his trademark pipe, Irving went about his business (which included reveling in the critics' lavish praise for his latest novel, *The Miracle*). But first, he dug into one of a wallful of filing cabinets, picked out a mimeographed biography of Sylvia, written when her first novel, *The Fountains*, was published in 1978, and gave it to me. I began to read.

Born in New York City. Parents owned mom and pop candy store (with soda fountain) in which I worked after school from the age of eleven until I graduated Theodore Roosevelt High School in the Bronx at sixteen. . . .

Fred Bernstein: Was it fun, hanging out in the store?

Sylvia Wallace: Fun? I had to put down my books every day and go behind the counter. I remember my mother saying, "Your sister's putting in more hours than you are." I recall making a chart to show her that wasn't true. I was eleven or twelve. I also cannot remember that the four of us ever sat down and had a meal together. Because the store was open every single day of the year, except Yom Kippur, when you didn't eat anyway.

FB: Did you love your mother?

SW: It's instinctive to love your mother. But when that love gets mixed up with maternal criticism and rejection, there is conflict. My mother was a highly intelligent, disappointed, frustrated, also highly neurotic woman.

FB: What was wrong with her life?

SW: A lot of things. Her own mother committed suicide when she was thirteen. She came home from school one day and found a crowd outside the house. My mother loved me as well as she could love anyone, but because of her own tragedy as a child, she didn't have the capacity to give love freely.

FB: Not even to your father?

SW: It was not a love match. She often told me that she married my father because she wanted someone who would be good to her. It was very sad. She was born in Hartford, Connecticut and he had come over from what was then Austria. In arguments, she would mimic his accent. It was painful for all of us.

FB: So did you dream of getting out of the Bronx?

SW: It wasn't a dream—it was a need.

I continue reading Sylvia's biography.

. . . *Have never revisited the Bronx. Growing up experience too traumatic. In 1973, felt able to cope, and asked taxi driver to take me to scenes of my childhood. He refused. Said it was too dangerous.* . . .

FB: Really, you never went back?

SW: For a long time after I came to California, I couldn't remember where I was raised, where I went to school. I just dropped my own Iron Curtain and started over.

. . . *Had always dreamed of being part of the publishing world. Took a job at Dell Publishing. Weeks later, was plucked from mailroom and transferred to editorial.* . . .

FB: You didn't want to go to college?

SW: It never even occurred to me to try. That was for other people. I had been groomed to be a secretary/bookkeeper.

. . . Became a Miss Lonelyhearts of sorts, answering mail from readers with problems. Soon moved on to copywriter. Then Dell sent me to Hollywood to become their West Coast editor, making me, at eighteen, the youngest editor in the U.S. . . .

SW: It was wonderful to be free. I couldn't believe where I was. I had never been anywhere. It was like a dream. They told me to buy myself a new car and send the bill to them. I did—I bought a new blue Chrysler. They told me to get an apartment, so I did. It was the first time I'd ever had my own space.

FB: What became of your parents?

SW: I encouraged them to move out here. It seemed to me that a change like that would make them happier. I didn't realize it was a lost cause.

. . . Was in charge of magazines, principally Dell's Hollywood flagship, Modern Screen. *Trip to coast was notable for several reasons. It was the first time I had traveled west of the Hudson River; I met Cary Grant; I met Irving Wallace. . . .*

FB: Was Irving famous when you met him?

SW: No. He was a young free-lance magazine writer, living with his parents.

. . . Married June 1941. Following two-month honeymoon (Mexico, Cuba), returned to Dell and continued as West Coast editor until 1947. Left Dell. . . .

FB: What happened?

SW: Irving was discharged from the service and he was again writing articles. He had to travel—so I gave up my job to go with him.

. . . In 1948, first child, David Wallechinsky (né Wallace) was born. Settled into full-time motherhood, which, for me, was a disaster. A convocation of doctors: internist, psychiatrist, obstetrician, pediatrician, put me together again, assuring me it was all right, in fact, necessary, for me to be a working mother. . . .

FB: You were lucky that your doctors were so understanding.

SW: Either I was lucky or they didn't know what else to do with me.

FB: You were that bad off?

SW: I'd cracked up.

FB: Literally?

SW: Literally. It went beyond boredom. I was sick. I couldn't get out of bed.

FB: How did the people around you react?

SW: My mother told me I was no mother. She saw me sick, and that's what she said. What she didn't realize was that all those years she had spent in the candy store she too was a working woman who enjoyed outside stimulation.

FB: And Irving?

SW: Irving was not sympathetic about my returning to work. He simply did not understand my need for activity outside the home. But he's come a long way.

FB: What do you think about that period now?

SW: I still get mad. There is absolutely no doubt: I was born at the wrong time. Now I would work all the way through.

. . . Returned gradually to adult world, ghostwriting magazine pieces for likes of Hedda Hopper and Sheilah Graham, who considered my writing some of the best they had ever done. In 1954, returned to full-time editorial work as West Coast editor of Photoplay *magazine. Worked with actors daily, among them Marilyn Monroe, Frank Sinatra, Lauren Bacall, Rock Hudson, Elizabeth Taylor, Ronald Reagan. . . .*

FB: Tell me about Reagan.

SW: He was a bore. He got the latest *Reader's Digest* before everybody else, and he spouted it for weeks. He's still doing it.

. . . Daughter Amy born in 1955. . . .

FB: This time, did you continue working?

SW: Amy was born practically at my desk. She was premature. I had to leave her in the hospital incubator for twelve days. I felt great, so, with the blessing of her pediatrician, I went back to work.

FB: Did you feel guilty?

SW: Of course. Every minute.

. . . Continued as working mother with two children for a couple of years until whole thing became too much to handle. Societal pressures were tremendous—so I quit job. . . .

FB: Couldn't you resist those pressures?

SW: I know now that I didn't have the self-esteem that carried many other women. I didn't have enough self-confidence to follow my own star. And I had a mother-in-law who said of me, "You dream and dream about the kind of girl your son is going to marry, and then he brings her home, and you try to make the best of it." Poor lady. She never understood that women could be individuals.

FB: How did you spend your time at home?

SW: I began to cut recipes out of magazines, I bought a toolbox and did minor carpentry, and I arranged flowers.

FB: Did David like it better when you were home?

SW: No. He liked it less. He said, "Why did you ever quit?" He was telling me I didn't need to feel guilty. Now when I talk to other mothers who are torn, I tell them about David. Quitting work is my one major regret.

FB: Were you sorry you had children?

SW: No! No! I wanted the kids. They are the greatest thing that ever happened to me. I have always loved them intensely.

FB: You said your mother couldn't love you fully. How did you manage to be so loving?

SW: I think when I met Irving, I took a chance on love. And the gamble paid off. From then on, love was free-flowing.

. . . Husband changed his own career, turning from screen-writing at studios to book-writing at home. Thus, as research aide and editor of his books, I was able to become reinvolved in publishing and be a full-time mother. . . .

FB: You edit Irving's writing?

SW: Yes. In those days, I line-edited the galleys. Now there are other people to do that, but I'm still the first to read and comment on his books. He wants my input. He takes what he considers valid and discards what he doesn't.

FB: Do you know what his books are about before they're written?

SW: Only in the broadest outline. For instance, we went to Berlin last year. I took notes, I took pictures—so I know the backgrounds, but very little of the scenes and characters.

. . . Have enjoyed many privileges: satisfaction with husband's success, interesting spectrum of friends, frequent travels to beloved places like London, Paris, and, best of all, Venice. But at same time, felt personal identity washing away. Admirers of Irving Wallace books edged me into corners; at parties, guests met me for sixth time and never remembered the other five. Once engaged in three-way conversation with Betty Friedan. I asked questions, she responded to Irving. . . .

FB: What were your ambitions for your children?

SW: I didn't have time for any. It was the sixties. The horror of Vietnam, and drugs, were predominant in my mind.

FB: Were your kids very involved in drugs?

SW: I thought so. Of course, back then, I didn't know the difference between pot and heroin. It's funny: now they are so concerned with what goes into their bodies—both of them are vegetarians.

FB: How did the war affect them?

SW: Well, David was at UCLA—where he was restless and unhappy. The university was huge and he was not motivated to study. I was afraid he'd be dropped out—and then could be drafted. So behind his back I went to Santa Monica City College, which was smaller, and I registered him, so he wouldn't have even one day of exposure to the draft. Two years later he went to San Francisco State, where he spent the rest of his college career demonstrating. He didn't stay for a degree. Amy would never go to college at all—she knew she wanted to be a writer. So no one in this family has a degree.

FB: How involved were they in the antiwar movement?

SW: Enough to have been arrested during protest demonstrations in Miami.

FB: Were you upset about that?

SW: I would not have said, "Amy, lie down and get arrested," but I was sympathetic. With Vietnam, I was the first one on the block to say that something's wrong here.

FB: It sounds like you were a pretty liberal parent.

SW: I learned from the kids—really, they raised me. For instance, I learned from them not to immediately take an adversarial position in a political dispute—I try to hear the other person out, which is what they do. I don't try to control them—I just want to know that they're happy and safe and well.

FB: Did you get involved in their choice of mates?

SW: Not at all. David showed up with Flora and asked if she could live with him in our house. I said, "Ask your father." Irving said, "Ask your mother." It turned out we were both afraid of what the housekeeper would think.

FB: You were so nonchalant about it?

SW: I wasn't nonchalant. I just think it's wonderful that young people live together before they get married. I think a lot of divorces are avoided that way. David and Flora married because they love each other and because they wanted a child.

FB: What's Flora like?

SW: When David brought her home, he told me she was different. She was in that she was shy and had not had the intellectual exposure that David had had. But they have something much more basic: they understand each other's feelings.

FB: Why did David take the name Wallechinsky?

SW: It was a protest against Immigration changing anyone's name—Wallechinsky had been the family name until his grandfather got to Ellis Island. I still have trouble spelling it.

FB: It wasn't a return to his religion?

SW: No. Both our children married out of the Jewish faith. It was no problem for any of us. Flora is partly Navajo. They call their son, Elijah, the Nava-Jew.

. . . With children grown up, I found myself in classic dilemma. What now? Did not want to return to article-writing or editorial work—I'd been there. Had always been awed by books —they seemed impossible undertakings. But suddenly there was so much to say about women's changing roles—and I wanted to say it in a novel. A year and a half after it was begun, The Fountains *was completed. . . .*

FB: One would think, with your background, you would have written a first novel sooner.

SW: An interviewer asked me, "If you weren't Irving Wallace's wife, do you think you would have been published?" I said, "Yes, twenty years earlier."

FB: What stopped you?

SW: I just didn't think I could do it. I didn't think I could write. But Amy helped—she'd call up every day and say, "How's it going? What page are you on?"

FB: Your children were already successful. Were you jealous?

SW: On my honor: never. I've never been competitive with my children or my husband. I'm extremely proud of each of them. I kvell when they get good reviews.

FB: Did you ever help them with their writing?

SW: Well, I used to criticize Amy. But it was very mother-daughterish, and it was difficult for me to deal with her reaction, which was like, "You're not telling me what to do." But that's all gone. She brought me four chapters from her new book, *The Prodigy*—it's about William Sidis, the boy genius who entered Harvard at eleven. It's a joy to be able to say how terrific she is.

. . . *Collaborated with my family on* The Book of Lists 2. . . .

FB: How did you get involved in that?

SW: Well, they were working together. And at first I didn't want to join in, because I never wanted people to say I was riding on Irving's coattails. That was my "I've got to do it all myself" period. But they were giggling away in Irving's study. I thought they were having all the fun. So then I said okay, the hell with pride. I didn't have to prove anything anymore.

FB: What was it like to collaborate with your family?

SW: Wonderful. It was convivial—it was like my magazine days. I still like being in an office. We all rewrote each other—with no problem.

FB: So you got along well?

SW: Fantastically well. If there's one thing in Irving's and my life that's successful, it's the family. To raise children who don't hate you is an accomplishment.

FB: Did they ever hate you?

SW: I certainly hope so. I believe if a kid doesn't erupt early, he'll erupt later. There's got to be a breakaway.

. . . In June 1980, my second novel, Empress, *was brought out by Morrow. Again, joined my husband, son, daughter in doing* The Intimate Sex Lives of Famous People. *. . .*

FB: What was it like working on that book?

SW: Some of the writing was painful for me. I did a section on famous homosexuals. It took me three weeks to write two paragraphs on Bill Tilden, because I became emotionally involved in his suffering—his dying in disgrace.

FB: What else do you remember about *Sex Lives?*

SW: Really nothing. I'm not the kind of person who can tell you what was on page 348, line 16. I'm so on to the next thing.

. . . Now working on my third novel. . . .

FB: Do you have a publisher already?

SW: No. My agent wanted me to have a contract with a strict deadline, but I didn't want the pressure. Fortunately, I'm not a hungry writer.

. . . A one-time collector (art, objets), now on way to becoming ardent discarder, paring down, freeing self for other interests: writing, politics, skiing, travels to favorite European cities and escapist visits to nearby Malibu Beach hideaway and family farmhouse on tiny Balearic island of Menorca.

FB: You've accomplished a lot.

SW: By far the most important thing we've accomplished in our lives is having two great children. It's our only real achievement.

A couple of days after I interviewed her, Sylvia called me. She'd obviously been doing a lot of thinking.

SW: I checked with my children, and they do love me.

Richard Dreyfuss' mother

GERRY DREYFUSS

"RICHARD IS NOT ONLY AN ACTOR. HE FEELS
THINGS. HE HELPS OUT WITH GOOD CAUSES."

An air of loneliness hangs over Gerry Dreyfuss' apartment. It is
in the kind of Los Angeles neighborhood where pedestrians are
suspect, where one never sees a human being unshielded by
glass. It is filled with things salvaged from a house in which a
decades-long marriage went sour, and with mementos of
friends and relatives who are, in many cases, living thousands of
miles away.

But speak to Gerry Dreyfuss and the image of a lonely
divorcée with an inert existence turns out to be just a dead-
wrong first impression. Gerry is a fighter who survived the
breakup of her marriage ("We do a lot of that in California," she
says wryly), who defeated thyroid cancer, and who kept her
head when her son Richard was nearly killed in a car crash in
October 1982. It was in the wake of that accident that Richard
was charged with coke possession, and Gerry found out that her
son, "unbeknownst to me, was addicted to pills and liquor."

Worst of all, Gerry was forced to come to that realization in
public. "The news went all over the world," she says. "I've
loved having millions of people share the *naches*. Well, this time
they shared the pain."

Gerry says she's never stopped being proud of her son. "I
haven't met anyone yet who doesn't admire his work," she says.
"But it's important that Richard is not only an actor. He feels

things. He helps out with good causes. He works for Amnesty International. He read the poetry of the refuseniks at Madison Square Garden." Now he lectures to high school students about the dangers of cocaine and helps raise funds for drug abuse prevention. Says Gerry, "Every time I go over to his house, I see awards from organizations I didn't even know about. He's not a passive person, which is great."

Richard inherited a lot of that from Gerry, who he remembers from his childhood "was always trying to get signatures to save the Rosenbergs." These days, she belongs to "every peace group in L.A." and is working "to save the people of El Salvador."

Figures Richard's mother, "If you're going to live in this world, you have to be passionate about something."

She is passionate about *many* things. While her husband was fighting in World War II—he was seriously wounded in the Battle of the Bulge—Gerry helped form an organization called Wives to Get Soldiers Overseas the Vote. "It was the first time I was called a Communist," she says, "but it was definitely not the last." In 1958, she began working "to stop the city of L.A. from spending millions of dollars on air raid shelters, which only give false security. People told me to go back to Russia where I came from."

Actually, Gerry was born in Brooklyn—as were her parents. But their parents were immigrants from Riga. Her father was a Shell Oil salesman who, according to Gerry, "had to change his name from Rabinowitz to Robbins to get the job and keep it." For a time the family lived in eastern Pennsylvania. It was there that Gerry had her first encounter with anti-Semitism. "We had a little girl over once for Friday night dinner. My mother lit shabbes candles and explained what that meant. Later, we walked the girl home. By the time we got back to the house, the phone was ringing. My mother spoke to her mother. And then she said, 'I don't think that girl is going to be playing with you anymore.' "

Gerry raised her own three children first in Brooklyn, then in Bayside, Queens. But in 1956, when Richard was nine, she talked her husband into giving up his New York law practice and moving to L.A. She remembers, "We came out here to visit his brother, whose office looked out on palm trees. Norman's looked out on an airshaft at Forty-first and Broadway. Still, it took me three years to convince him."

It was also Gerry who decided, once the family had given up the apartment in New York, to take a six-month jaunt through Europe. "All three children were in school, but the teachers said, 'Take them. They'll learn more there.' Anyway, two weeks is the most you can ask somebody to watch your kids." So they flew to Europe, settled into a 1948 Citroën, complete with guitars and a birdcage (the bird soon died, but the cage stayed on top of the car), and set out on a transcontinental adventure. "My friends couldn't get over our courage," she says. "But think of the courage of our grandparents, who left the old country to make a new life here. We were just going to visit."

Richard, Gerry recalls, was a nonconformist from the start. "He was a boy who didn't care about the things boys are supposed to care about. He never hit anybody in anger. He was called a sissy by his friends. In the fourth grade, he said, 'Why is it, if I don't know batting averages, I'm a sissy? I know all about the Civil War!' He used to cry about it."

Still, he was "a very lovable child. Richard was a charmer. In restaurants," Gerry says, "he'd flirt with the waitresses, and they'd give him extra ice cream. At home, I'd have to pin a note to his shirt that said, 'Don't feed me,' or he'd go from apartment to apartment looking hungry. He was always chubby."

She remembers, "There was no question that he was going to be an actor. He first said so when he was five or six." Gerry encouraged him. "You can't stop anybody from doing what they want to do. As long as he stayed in school and did his work, I didn't see any reason why he shouldn't be an actor."

Richard's first role was Haman in a synagogue Purim pageant. Later he played Zionist statesman Theodor Herzl, and on Hanukkah he was "the ghost of an Assyrian soldier who kept blowing out the menorah." It was the drama—not the religion—that motivated him. "I remember him telling the rabbi that there is no God," says Gerry.

Richard was valedictorian of his elementary school graduating class. Gerry remembers, "His was not a 'this-is-not-the-end-it-is-a-grand-and-glorious-beginning' kind of speech. He chastised the parents. He bawled them out. He said they owed their children more than food and lodging—they had to prepare their children to make a better world. I was as shocked as anyone, but it got him a standing ovation."

At Beverly Hills High School, Richard couldn't pass math. "He got a D, so he took it again," Gerry says, "and he got an F. That's hard to do." But he was popular enough to run for class president—and lose. "There were four hundred more ballots cast than there were students," Gerry recalls, "and he demanded that the principal conduct a recount." Remembers Gerry, "The principal said to him, 'Oh, that's politics,' and he was shocked."

In college, he majored in drama—but he was forced to change departments after he got into a fight with his instructor over whether Marlon Brando was the greatest living actor. Then, as a conscientious objector during Vietnam, he took three years off from school to work as a file clerk at L.A. General Hospital, his "alternative public service." Gerry remembers that "on the day he told me he was going to file for conscientious objector status, I was very scared—and very proud."

Richard's first professional role was as "Hymie, the bar mitzvah boy," in a play called *Mama's House.* "I was bar mitzvahed every night for six months," he remembers. Then he graduated to TV, where he began appearing on such shows as *Judd for the Defense* and *Room 222.* Eventually he hit it big with a string of successful movies: *American Graffiti, The Apprenticeship of Duddy Kravitz, Jaws, Close Encounters of the Third Kind,* and *The Goodbye Girl.*

Gerry is a fan of those early pictures. *"Graffiti, Jaws,* and *Goodbye* are my favorites. *Duddy* wasn't bad." Gerry dismisses the charge that *Duddy Kravitz,* in portraying its title character in an unfavorable light, encouraged anti-Semitic feelings. "The fact that a Jew has to develop instincts for surviving that a WASP doesn't have to develop may make some of the things he does not so nice. But he is no less nice because he is a Jew than if he wasn't Jewish. There is a Duddy Kravitz in everyone." According to Gerry, Richard accepted invitations from many synagogues in the L.A. area to speak in defense of Duddy.

The Goodbye Girl caused no such problems. After it opened, Gerry recalls, "Every time we'd walk down the street, someone would say, 'Hey, Richard, how ya' doin'?' I've never seen such rapport between an actor and street people in New York." The family, which had pronounced its name "Drayfuss" since World War II, more and more went with "Dryfuss," the pronunciation Richard had adopted.

Gerry saw *Jaws* for the first time in a screening room full of theater owners, and she remembers, "When it was over, they knew they had a hit." After that, Gerry and her husband saw the film dozens of times. "Every night, if we felt like it, we'd walk over to the local theater and the manager would let us stand in the back—just for the scene, at eight forty-five, where the head falls off the boat. Everyone in the theater screamed. I loved it."

She has more trouble with some of his recent efforts. In *The Competition,* she says, "he was totally out of control. He needs a strong director, and when he doesn't have one, it shows." As for *Whose Life Is It, Anyway?,* Gerry says, "Richard is such a physical actor. And in this, playing a paraplegic, he couldn't move for the entire picture. You can tell that he was under a terrible strain."

As Richard's career took off, Gerry was building a successful business selling kitchen gadgets in department stores. "I can sell anybody anything in a crowd," she says. "If I can gather a crowd I can make them want to buy." Then, in 1970, she learned she had cancer. "I thought I was dying," she remembers. By now a divorcée, she sold her business, moved closer to her sister, and "for the first time in my life, I became a housewife. I gained forty pounds, which I haven't lost yet—not one ounce." She became reinvolved in the peace movement while remaining close to Richard, daughter Cathy, a public defender in L.A., and son Lorin, a screenwriter. "I'm not a lonely, abandoned woman," Gerry says.

Gerry doesn't go to the movies much anymore. "Too many

have the violence, sexism, and machismo which perpetuate all that rotten stuff in society." But she did get to try her own hand at directing—sort of—when Richard married Jeramie Rain, then a CBS producer. After the private ceremony, which the rabbi ended Hollywood-style by saying, "It's a wrap," Gerry threw a party for seven hundred people on a Warner Bros. soundstage. "The entire place was decorated like New York— there was a skyline in the background, and subway kiosks, and hot dog stands. People told me if I put all that together I could have done *Jaws.*"

Richard's marriage came as a complete surprise. "He met Jeramie on January seventh, became engaged on January tenth, and wanted to marry her on March twentieth." It also came during the most hectic period in his life—shortly after his arraignment for possession of cocaine and the painkiller Percodan, drugs Richard later admitted were messing up his life.

But Gerry says, "Jeramie is the best thing that's ever happened to this family. Richard has turned his entire personality around. He's madly in love. He is absolutely walking on air because of her."

Richard is equally enthralled with Emily Robin, his nineteen-month-old daughter. "Every day he announces what Emily did yesterday," says Gerry. "He claimed she came running out one night and said, ' 'Bye, Daddy, see you in the morning.' Now do you think she really said that?"

Then Gerry jokes, "Actually, she's reciting the Gettysburg Address and flying her own Learjet. Otherwise, she's just an ordinary baby."

Richard's latest film, *Down and Out in Beverly Hills,* co-stars Bette Midler—and Gerry Dreyfuss. Director Paul Mazursky cast her in the role of Richard's mother. At first Gerry told Mazursky, "You must be kidding. I'm not an actress." But Mazursky hired her after a one-minute audition. Gerry spent three weeks on the set. "My only fear," she recalls, "was embarrassing Richard." But, in fact, she rarely got to see him. "I went into his dressing room for a mother-son chat, and after five minutes, he had to go somewhere and I had to go somewhere.

Acting is hard work. Now I know why they get paid as much as they do.

"Richard makes me very proud," adds Gerry. "I say to him, 'Could Laurence Olivier's mother possibly feel this good?'

"I doubt it."

Mitch Gaylord's mother

LINDA GAYLORD

"THE WOMAN WHO GETS HIM HAS GOT HERSELF SUCH A GEM."

It was one of the most dramatic moments of the 1984 Olympics. In the men's gymnastics finals, the U.S. team had a chance at a gold medal—its first since 1932. Mitch Gaylord, the high-bar virtuoso, was about to perform a maneuver called the Gaylord II, a move so tough that during training he missed it four out of ten times. Now, with the crowds at UCLA's Pauley Pavilion hushed, Gaylord took off into a flyaway back flip with a half twist. As *Sports Illustrated* put it, "For one flickering moment he was lost from view as he twisted in the lights. Then he came winging back down and as everybody did an 'Oh, my god,' he somehow stretched far beyond his 5'9" to grab the bar in time. He drew a 9.95, and that, Olympic fans, was that."

Gaylord's mother, Linda, says, "I cried when the team won. You couldn't help it." For five days, she had dreaded coming to Pauley Pavilion "the way you dread a doctor's appointment. I had to drag myself out there. It was really stressful. My husband lost ten pounds during the Olympics, and I'm sure I aged ten years. During the competition, there were times when I would rather have been anywhere else. But of course I had to be there."

Why the panic? During the weeks before the games, "it was looking bleak," remembers Linda. The Gaylord II wasn't working. "He would miss twenty-five in a row. The time was drawing near. And I was afraid if he failed in the Olympics, he wouldn't come out feeling very good about himself. But Mitch is very motivated by his stomach. Chuck [Mitch's older brother and gymnastics coach] would promise him a dinner in a restaurant if he'd catch three in a row. That helped."

At home, Linda and Fred Gaylord kept their worries to themselves. "The trick," Linda says, "was to act as nonchalant and confident around Chuck and Mitch as we could." Most of the time, they didn't even talk about the Olympics. "There had to be some respite from it. The house became a sanctuary for them."

It didn't stay that way for long. With Mitch's sudden fame, the family was besieged. Phone calls came at all hours of the night. So did uninvited guests. "One girl hitchhiked here from Georgia," Linda says. "She went to UCLA, and they gave her the address." Understandably, Linda keeps the location of Mitch's new apartment under wraps. "We've given up on this location," she says of her house in Van Nuys (in the San Fernando Valley). "It's been discovered. There's no reason why Mitch should have the same thing."

Still, there are other reminders of his popularity. His apartment is stacked up with cartons of mail—17,000 letters at last count. Says Linda, "Some went to ABC. Some went to the Olympic Village. Some went to 'Mitch Gaylord, c/o Peter Ueberroth.' A lot went to UCLA. Some even went to the Stephen Wise Temple, because they read that we belong there."

The boys who write are usually very sports-minded. Some are small for their ages—they write because they've read that Mitch was only five foot two when he graduated from high school. (He's since added seven inches, a phenomenal amount of growth after eighteen. Says Linda, "The kids who went to high school with him, then saw him in the Olympics, were completely shocked.")

If the letters are from girls, they're probably the same girls who buy the teen magazines that feature Mitch month after month. Linda has a stack of the magazines in her den. "Mitch is embarrassed to be a hunk and a teen idol," she says. "But he knows these are the same people who come to see him." Then she adds, "The human body is a beautiful thing. Why not show it off if you've got a nice one? And Mitch has a very nice one."

Mitch plans to answer every letter; he has declined to turn the cartons over to gymnastics organizations that have offered to handle the task because, as Linda says, "he likes to be involved in everything that concerns him." In the meantime, Linda and a "support network" of relatives have screened the letters, turning over to Mitch any from "people with truly unfortunate stories. Those Mitch answers right away."

Mitch is genuinely concerned about his fans. When he was sixteen, Linda says, "He attended a gymnastics meet in Pasadena, and one of his idols was there. And the guy snubbed Mitch; he wouldn't give him the time of day. That's when Mitch decided that whenever anyone came up to him, he would make eye contact, do something that says, 'You're a person too.' " But without Pasadena, she adds, "He would have done it anyway, because he's a good person."

A Los Angeles native, Linda Troop met Fred Gaylord in high school. They started dating when she was thirteen and he fifteen, and they married five years later. "I never went out with another boy," says Linda. "It was a given that we would marry. My parents just hoped I'd get my diploma first."

Fred was a boxboy at a local supermarket when they married. The plan was for Linda to work while Fred went to college. "But I got pregnant right away." Chuck was born when Linda was nineteen ("we sold one of our cars to pay the hospital"). Mitch arrived when she was twenty-one. (Jeanine, now a student at Stanford, came along five years later.) "My friends would come home from college and try to sympathize with my plight," says Linda. "They didn't understand how much I loved my situation. I think I was born to parent."

She took the job seriously enough. "We were out to prove to the world that we were old enough to have kids, so we were tough disciplinarians," says Linda. "We weren't wishy-washy parents."

Nor was Mitch a wishy-washy child. "The fact that his brother was nineteen months older didn't seem to mean anything to him," says Linda. "He pushed himself to do everything Chuck did. He was totally competitive. When he was four, he learned to ride a twenty-inch bicycle. The only way he could stop it was to crash."

As a result, says Linda, "Mitch was incredibly accident-prone. He was at the UCLA emergency room so much, they looked at us like we were child abusers. He split his scalp open when he was two and a half. When he was three, he o.d.'d on aspirin. He rode through a barbed wire fence at eight or nine, then he bit his tongue through playing tetherball." Adds Linda, "He gave us a lot of excitement well before the Olympics."

As soon as he could, Mitch played Little League and flag football. "The whole family got involved," says Linda. "But then he got outsized. My husband sat down with him and said, 'You've got to pick a sport where size isn't important.'"

Linda says of Mitch's days as the smallest boy in his grade, "I think he gained from it; I really do. I think he is less judgmental of others. He doesn't go by appearances. He just gained in humility. It obviously didn't stop him."

When Mitch took up gymnastics, "His first love was the trampoline," says Linda, adding, "If I had known then what I know now about how dangerous it was, I might have a few more gray hairs." But she wouldn't have stood in his way.

"Gymnastics gave Mitch direction; it gave him discipline," says Linda. "Until then, he was a free spirit." Linda adds that Mitch was an above-average student—"but he didn't work at it. Whole semesters would go by without him bringing home any books. Fred and I were always on his case. When he was sixteen, he told Chuck, 'I'm real sorry Mom and Dad are upset about my grades. But my future is gymnastics.'"

Mitch began competing while attending public school in Van Nuys. ("Now," says Linda, "they all claim him: 'He went to this school.' 'No, he went to that school.'") His first success on an international level came during the Maccabiah Games (the "Jewish Olympics") in Israel in 1981. "We all went," says Linda, "and it was the most moving experience of our lives. Of course it helped that Chuck and Mitch walked away with every gymnastics gold medal."

At the World Games in Moscow in 1982, Mitch was still in the competition after the entire Israeli team had been eliminated. "So they adopted him," says Linda. "Suddenly, there was a whole section cheering for Mitch. He considers himself an American first, but he's very proud to be Jewish.

"He cried at his bar mitzvah," Linda remembers. Then, when he was sworn in by the President's Council on Physical Fitness (he is now its youngest member), "it reminded him of his bar mitzvah," Linda says. "He didn't cry, but he told me he came very close." Adds Linda, "Mitch is a very unusual person. He's strong but he's not afraid to be emotional. The woman who gets him has got herself such a gem."

In her comfortable living room, Linda shows me some of the mementos of Mitch's career, including his four Olympics medals (after the team won the gold, Mitch picked up three individual medals—one silver and two bronze). Says Linda, "Mitch is very modest. He hasn't worn them since he got them."

She shows me pictures of her son with Ronald and Nancy Reagan, taken after he joined the President's Council. She shows me a videotape of Mitch's Olympics high-bar routine. "Even though I know how it comes out," she says, "I still get a knot in my stomach." And then she shows me a videotape of Mitch's screen test, which landed him the starring role in *American Anthem* opposite Janet *(The Flamingo Kid)* Jones. "He's working with an acting coach," says Linda. "He's such an easygoing, mellow guy, and now for this role he's got to be able to scream and yell and pound his fist on the table." But she's sure Mitch can do it. After all, "Putting on a show for eleven thousand people in an arena is a performance." Within a year, Mitch Gaylord the gold medalist may be Mitch Gaylord the movie star.

Linda doesn't think that would change her son. The gold medals haven't. "He still takes out the garbage and walks the dog," she says. Moreover, "He refuses to be the center of attention during family dinners. When he comes to dinner, which is whenever you invite him—and I mean whenever—he does not want to be the focus of conversation. We actually called the family before one Thanksgiving and said, 'Gymnastics is off-limits.' We feel all three of our children are equally successful. It's just that Mitch's accomplishments make the papers."

Even now that Mitch has taken his own apartment, Linda sees him often. Chuck and Mitch still hold her hand when they walk together, she says. "They also like to pick me up. They think it's real cute that I'm not too tall."

Linda runs an international folk dancing group ("with emphasis on Israeli") at a local synagogue. She also directs a children's dance troupe that performs around the community, and she works five days a week as an aide at a local kindergarten.

Linda says she loves her work, but she adds, "I always wanted to be a mother and a housewife and a wife. If I did not have a so-called career as a dance teacher, I would still feel I'd accomplished something special with my life. And not only because of Mitch."

Marilyn Michaels' mother

FRAYDELE OYSHER

"SHE TRIED TO IMITATE ME ONCE. I TOLD HER, 'IF I
EVER SEE YOU DOING THAT AGAIN, I'LL BREAK
YOUR ASS.'"

Marilyn Michaels is the most successful female impressionist
ever—and it's no wonder. She can sing as well as Barbra, drawl
as well as Dinah, tell a joke as well as Joan. How else could she so
convincingly impersonate all three?

So on-target are Marilyn's impressions that celebrities are
usually flattered to become her subjects. "I know I've finally
arrived," Julie Andrews once said, "now that Marilyn Michaels
has done me."

Of course, not all of her subjects are so gracious. "She tried
to imitate me once," recalls Fraydele Oysher. "I told her, 'If I
ever see you doing that again, I'll break your ass.'"

Fraydele Oysher, Marilyn's mother, was one of the great
stars of the Yiddish theater. Born in Lipkon, Bessarabia (now
part of the U.S.S.R.), she came to New York as an infant with her
mother and her brother, Moishe Oysher. Together, she and
Moishe were the Shirley MacLaine and Warren Beatty of their
era: he a dashing leading man (and world-renowned cantor),
she a singer-actress who toured the world as "The Israelite
Sensation" in shows written especially for her.

It's been decades since Fraydele Oysher appeared on the
Yiddish stage. But her greatest performance was not given until
last year. The audience was me.

There were clues that it was coming. "Marilyn told me you would call," said Fraydele over the phone. "I said to her, 'You probably want me to tell him that you were a dear, sweet, loving child. Well, forget it.' "

Still, I didn't expect that during a three-hour interview Fraydele would run through the entire range of emotions of every part she's ever played, and then some. But then I didn't know Fraydele Oysher, a five-foot-nothing powerhouse who wears her talent on her sleeve. One second she is curled up in the back of an oversized chair, playing the little girl. The next second, she has leaped up and, using every muscle in her body, is reenacting the dramatic moments of her tragedy-filled life.

She is also very funny. "I'd sell my husband to the Arabs for a laugh," she warns me as the interview begins, and I believe her. Periodically, her husband, Harold Sternberg, a Metropolitan Opera basso, enters the room. "What are we, twins?" she demands after he has merely said "Hello." "We have separate rooms," she adds, "but we ought to have separate countries."

But forget Harold: Fraydele is ready to talk about Marilyn. "So you want to know about Marilyn?" she asks me at the door. "Well, I'll tell you about Marilyn. She's rich. She's famous. She's talented. And she's a pain in the behind."

In no time, Fraydele is listing her complaints about her daughter.

She didn't become an opera singer: When Marilyn first began singing, Harold's friends advised him that she had as great a vocal range as anyone except Joan Sutherland, Fraydele says. So did she take up opera? "That I can't even bring myself to talk about."

She insisted on doing impressions: "I wanted her to go into the legitimate theater. I said, 'I didn't die a thousand deaths for this.' True, you don't get paid as much on Broadway as in nightclubs and TV. But she didn't have to support me the way I had to support my mother."

She doesn't listen: "I'm telling you, if she had taken my advice, she'd be bigger than Barbra. Why? Because—this is the key—Barbra is always Barbra."

She's not famous enough: "Isn't Marilyn a big enough star?" I ask. Fraydele answers, "For her talent, no.

"Of course," Fraydele interjects, "none of this career stuff is important. What really matters is, how is she as a person? How is she to her father and me?"

"Well," I ask, "how is she?"

"Not so good," Fraydele answers.

And so the litany continues:

She doesn't call home enough: "It began when she started seeing a psychiatrist. She said her psychiatrist told her she had to be her own person. So now she's the psychiatrist's person."

She calls home too much: (During the interview, Marilyn phones from California, then says she has to go because there's someone at the door.) "Can you believe this? She calls me from California to say she has to go."

She spends too much money: "Her priorities are all screwed up. She thinks she's Dina Merrill."

She's too into herself: "I need to be involved in things. Like when they sent the space shuttle up, with those flies for experiments. I needed to know, were the flies floating, or did they have to fly? Do you think Marilyn cared? No. She said, 'Don't bother me with that.'"

She's not domestic: "People ask, 'What does she do?' and I say, 'Oh, she sings, she dances, she acts. But she doesn't cook.'"

She's immature: "I don't think anyone as talented as Marilyn can ever be completely mature."

Her material is too raunchy: "Do I approve? Does it matter whether I approve? Marilyn, don't forget, is a grown woman—chronologically."

At this point, Marilyn's mother begins to wonder if she's giving me enough material for my book. "Ask me some questions," she announces, "and I'll open up."

According to Fraydele, it was clear, from the day Marilyn was born, that she had talent. "It didn't have to be," she moans. "Look at Caruso's children; they were nothings. But it was."

And so the stage was set. Mother and daughter would soon

be locked in a power struggle that would make the 118-year-long Punic Wars seem puny.

As Fraydele tells it, Marilyn announced, when she was two, that she was going to be a star. "For a stick of gum, she would entertain you for an hour." And once, her mother says, she crawled out of her crib and into the street, where a car almost hit her. "She didn't care about that," says Fraydele. "What mattered was that the headlights were on her. Naturally, she started singing."

Things got worse when Marilyn was old enough to come to the theater when Fraydele was performing. Fraydele says, "Marilyn wanted to be on stage, like me. She had the best baby-sitters in the world—Molly Picon, Menasha Skolnick—and even they couldn't restrain her. I was never safe."

Once, Fraydele was doing a song—a serious song—when the audience started laughing. The men in the orchestra started checking their flies. "But it was Marilyn, standing behind me, conducting the orchestra with her six-inch-long arms," Fraydele groans.

"She was jealous," Fraydele goes on. "She thought I had too much adulation. Everyone else would say, 'You were great, Miss Oysher,' or 'You were wonderful, Miss Oysher,' and she would say, 'You were standing too close to the mike, Miss Oysher.'"

Fraydele says she wanted Marilyn to be like other girls, but it was hopeless. "She'd walk around saying, 'If you give me money, I'll give you a concert.' On the boardwalk at Coney Island, a man was photographing his children. And she said, 'Take one of me. I'm an actress.' And look how she posed," says Fraydele, going through a shoebox of old pictures. "Like Marilyn Monroe. Like Betty Grable. Is that normal for a four-year-old girl? I don't know where she got it."

Of course, Fraydele says, "It wasn't easy having me for a mother, either. I taught my kids to talk dirty when they were little, because I hate boring children. Luckily, Marilyn was anything but boring."

What were Fraydele's other faults as a mother? "Let's face it, Marilyn was very overprotected," Fraydele says. "But what are you going to do, if you have a diamond? Are you going to throw it around, dirty it, break it? No, you have to insure it!"

At seven, Marilyn landed her first role. "I wasn't a stage mother, trying to bask in her reflected glory. I was on the stage myself." In fact, Fraydele says, "I knew the heartbreaks. The tragedy was being in the same business—another mother would not have been so worried."

Still, she couldn't keep Marilyn out of showbiz. "She was accustomed to doing what she pleased—and getting away with it. And I had to let her. I was a performer. I needed my voice."

Eventually, though, Fraydele gave up her career. "I could have gone farther, but I didn't want my children [son Michael Sternberg is a teacher and musician] to be latchkey children. I wanted them to have more security than I had."

But it was too late. Fraydele says, "I wanted Marilyn to roller-skate, to go to proms. But it wasn't meant to be." By the time she got to the High School of Music and Art, Marilyn was so wrapped up in dramatics, Fraydele says, "that sometimes I thought I'd have to burn the place down to get her home." Yet academically, according to her mother, "she was a wipeout. Her teacher said, 'You flunked math,' and she said, 'So what? When I'm famous, I'll have an accountant.' "

Eventually, Fraydele came to accept what she could not change. "I told her, 'I don't want you to do this, but if you do, you have to do it better than anyone else in the world.' I wasn't easy to have as a mother."

She began giving Marilyn career advice, none of which was followed. "If I told her to do something, she wouldn't do it—just because I told her."

True, it was Fraydele who made Marilyn learn the score of *Funny Girl*. And it was Fraydele who, when she heard that Carol Lawrence, who was supposed to do *Funny Girl* on Long Island, had had an accident on *The Tonight Show*, went running down to Marilyn's apartment in a nightgown. "I said, 'Stand by your phone.' " When the call came, Fraydele, throwing a raincoat on over her nightgown, drove Marilyn directly to her first rehearsal.

And it was Fraydele who taught Marilyn to do one of her

best impressions. Because her *Kopykats* TV series was filmed in London, Marilyn had to do Edith Bunker before she'd ever seen *All in the Family.* But Fraydele, who had seen the program, described Edith over the phone. Marilyn's imitation was a smash.

As Marilyn became more and more famous, Fraydele became more and more nonchalant. "She'd say, 'This one was in my dressing room; that one was in my dressing room.' I said, 'When Helen Hayes is in your dressing room, then call me.' So she calls and says, 'Guess who's in my dressing room.' And I said, 'Marilyn, this is long distance. Let's not play games.' And she said, 'It's Helen Hayes.' And I said, 'Yeah, and I'm the Queen of Roumania.' "

It's not that Fraydele didn't want Marilyn to be famous. "People say, 'Aren't you proud?' Of course I'm proud. But I'm also full of anxieties." That's one reason Fraydele never goes to Marilyn's opening nights. "I don't want to be there to say, 'Oh, no.' It would be too much for both of us."

And then there are the memories of her own career. "When Marilyn was in *Funny Girl,* I took my mother to see her. And she turned around and said to me, in the most pathetic voice, 'Why do you let her work so hard?' She forgot that I—her own daughter—used to work five times as hard, for a dollar seventy-five a show."

These days, however, the tensions between mother and daughter seem to be subsiding. Fraydele is working again—she has acted in a number of commercials. And Fraydele and Marilyn have jointly recorded two stirring albums of Yiddish songs, produced by Harold. "Marilyn respects her heritage," Fraydele says.

Then there was Marilyn's wedding, in 1982, to Dr. Peter Wilk, which fulfilled one of Fraydele's lifelong dreams. She figures, "No woman is complete until she has someone to share with, even if it's only aggravation."

It's time for me to leave, and I am confused by what I've seen: jealousy, competition, guilt—and love. "I love Marilyn, desperately," Fraydele tells me.

"I know," I say, as I begin to walk out the door.

"Will you tell Marilyn?" Fraydele calls out to me as I am starting down the hall. "Tell Marilyn."

"I'm sure Marilyn knows."

"Uri Geller's mother

MARGARETTE GERO

"I'M GLAD THAT HE HAS THE POWER. BUT I'M
AFRAID. I DON'T WANT TO KNOW IF I CAN DO IT
TOO."

The living room of Uri Geller's New York apartment is littered
with improbably bent flatware, the remains of years of demonstrations of his psychic powers. Now he is about to bend my
housekey with the brute force of his mind. Smiling, Geller
places the key in the palm of his left hand, then gently strokes it
with the ordinary-looking index finger of his right. The idea, he
explains, is to transmit "psychic energy"—which he reportedly
possesses in overabundance—to the metal. I am skeptical; Geller seems confident as he administers a few more gentle
touches. Then, unceremoniously, he places the key on a table. It
is, just as he had predicted it would be, bent at an angle so
pronounced that I, saddled with ordinary mental powers, need
a hammer to unbend it.

My amazement is apparent; indeed, it is matched in inten-
sity only by the nonchalance of the jolly-faced lady perched on
Geller's sofa. Her expression voices the ultimate Jewish mother
protestation: "So? And why shouldn't my son have psychic powers?"

If Geller truly is psychic, his mother, Margarette Gero, long
ago learned to accept that which she cannot understand. If, on
the other hand, he is merely a highly skilled magician, she has
become part of his act. Speaking haltingly (English is not one of

the five languages in which Margarette is fluent), Uri Geller's mother tells of raising a son who was special even as an infant. She insists he could "see" things that he had no way of knowing. From the time he was old enough to play cards, she says, "He never lost. He always knew every card in my hand. And it was impossible to keep a secret from him. So I didn't even try." Indeed, if Uri habitually interrupts his mother, finishing her sentences in his polished English, Margarette does not object. After all, "Uri could always read my mind."

In that case, he must know before she says it that "at first, his powers scared me. But soon I got used to them." One reason: her father, a textile manufacturer in Berlin, was a first cousin of Sigmund Freud and "everyone in the family had a sixth sense." Margarette was no exception: as a child, she noticed that if she dreamed she had a toothache, someone close to her took sick. And if she dreamed that she was swimming in muddy water, a friend or relative was in some kind of trouble.

"She may have some kind of precognitive ability," explains Uri. But Margarette is content to write off her "powers" to superstition. (She *is* superstitious; she says she has never walked under a ladder or crossed a street after seeing a black cat.) And in seventy years, she has never tried to duplicate Uri's feats. "I'm glad," she says, "that he has the power. But I'm afraid. I don't want to know if I can do it too."

Her life has been hectic enough without that knowledge. Born outside Berlin, where she knew her famous cousin Sigmund "vaguely," Margarette was raised in Budapest, her mother's familial home. In 1938, already married to Uri's father, she fled to Palestine a few steps ahead of the Nazis. The rest of her family remained in Hungary, and, sheltered by Christian friends, survived the war. Though Margarette occasionally received news from home through other refugees, it wasn't until 1957 that she was able to communicate with her family directly.

She had a lot to tell them. Forced by her husband to undergo repeated abortions, Margarette was childless until her late thirties. Then she rebelled. "I wanted to have someone," is her simple explanation for defying her husband. The result: Uri was born and, soon after, her husband left her. Margarette remarried on Cyprus, snatching one year of "total happiness" before her second husband died, leaving her to run his pensione. Uri helped out when he wasn't at the local Catholic school. (He remembers, "Even the bushes were planted in the shape of a cross"—but it was the best school in the city.) He also spied on the pensione guests, a number of whom claimed to be archaeologists from a university in Israel. Uri guessed (or, as he puts it, "felt psychically") that they were really agents of the Israeli CIA. When he confronted them with his suspicions, the agents hired Uri to deliver letters and "do other cloak-and-dagger stuff."

At seventeen, Uri returned home to Israel to join the paratroopers. Injured in the Six Day War, he took up modeling. "My only goal," he says, "was to buy my mother a TV." Soon he was on TV demonstrating his psychic powers. Professors swore by him, diplomats (including Abba Eban) and generals invited him to perform at their homes, and Air Force pilots consulted with him before undertaking dangerous missions.

Once the initial excitement wore off, Margarette began feeling uncomfortable in Israel. "Some of my friends became jealous, because their children didn't have such powers." But Uri was already conquering the world. In Germany, he appeared on the cover of *Der Spiegel,* and in Japan, after he "broadcast" his powers over TV, thousands of viewers claimed to see their spoons bend. In the United States, he became a regular on talk shows and the college lecture circuit. Even the Pentagon hired him, reportedly to try to counter Soviet efforts to use ESP to determine the locations of nuclear warheads.

Not everyone was convinced. Magicians claimed to be able to duplicate his feats, and science magazines debunked him. That may explain why Geller has given up performing. Instead, he claims, he now uses his powers to discover gold and oil. Such activities, he says, have increased his net worth to tens of millions of dollars. He lives with his wife and two children—he says the kids have inherited some of his powers—on an estate in the English countryside. Margarette, who occupies a guest house, says, "He gives me everything I want." Indeed, she complains, pointing to her oversized diamond stud earrings, "I have too much."

Now Uri is attempting to read my mind. On a pad that he can't see, I draw a simple outline of the AT&T Building, the unusually shaped Manhattan skyscraper that I'm not even sure he'd recognize. Uri tells me to concentrate on what I've drawn. I do. He shuts his eyes, then starts to speak, then stops, then starts again. "I just can't get it," he announces. Is he really stuck, or is he heightening the drama? Then he says, "I keep getting confused between 'telephone' and 'building.' I'm sorry."

Sorry? I am awed, but Margarette, once again, is nonchalant.

Yakov Smirnoff's mother

CLARA SMIRNOFF

"THE FREEDOM HERE IS UNBELIEVABLE. IN RUSSIA, WE WERE ASHAMED TO SAY THAT WE ARE JEWISH."

> People don't realize there are comedians in Russia. They're dead, but they're there. . . . There was a contest for the best political joke. First prize: twenty years. . . . In Russia, you have to choose your material carefully. If you say, "Take my wife, please," when you get home, she's gone. . . . And if someone heckles you in Russia, it doesn't work to yell, "Your mother wears army boots," because she probably does. . . .
>
> —Yakov Smirnoff, Russian emigré comic

To make it as a comedian in one's own country is hard. To make it as a comedian in a foreign country—which means perfecting the nuances, the cadence, of a strange language—would seem impossible. But the impossible is exactly what Yakov Smirnoff has done. Until eight years ago, he was a successful stand-up comic in the Soviet Union. Then he moved to the United States. Smirnoff quickly established himself as one of the top young comedians in the country—he became a regular at Caroline's in New York, the Improvisation in L.A., and other comedy clubs between the coasts; he made more than a dozen appearances on TV; and he landed a small role in Robin Williams' movie *Moscow on the Hudson*. That led to parts in two other films, *The Adventures of Buckaroo Banzai* and Richard Pryor's *Brewster's Millions*. Smirnoff's previous acting experience? "I tried to act happy in Russia."

So dead-on is Smirnoff's delivery, so right-on is his satire of life in these United States, that he is constantly accused of only pretending to be foreign. "My friends say, 'You're really an American, right? Come on, you can tell me.'"

But Yakov Smirnoff is as Russian as his name—and for proof, one need only visit his mother, Clara. I did—and was treated to a meal of blintzes filled with chicken and kasha, stuffed cabbage and peppers, and borscht. (Joked Yakov, "We couldn't eat over there, so we're making up for lost time.") After we ate, Clara presented me with a tiny samovar, one of the few possessions she was allowed to take out of Russia. (I protested, but Clara insisted I accept the gift. "I'm very proud of this interview," she told me.)

Clara is gradually becoming Americanized. Her English is better than it was, and she is wearing a necklace that says "#1 MOTHER" (a present, naturally, from Yakov). And she is as addicted to *The Young and the Restless* and *As the World Turns* as any homegrown housewife.

But unlike her son, who eight years after his arrival on these shores owns a house in the Hollywood Hills and a Rolls-Royce, Clara still feels out of place. She says bluntly, "Yakov is very good, and very patient. But he doesn't understand all our problems."

The biggest is the language barrier. Clara has a hard time holding a conversation without a Russian-English dictionary. "I like to talk to Americans, but they have no patience," she says. "I'm ashamed to talk with American people. I need to communicate. That is the worst part about the immigration. In Russia I was a full person."

Then, too, Clara misses her relatives back home. Though she writes to her sister, she says, "I can only talk about my high pressure, the weather—nothing else. And I ask not one question. I'm very careful. I'm so afraid about them. It's impossible for Americans to understand. Only my sister, because she's retired, can go to the post office for the letter. My nephew cannot go there." And Clara is afraid to phone.

"Yakov's happy, and we are proud," says Clara. "And my husband is so happy here. He feels free. I am lucky with them. But for me, I can't explain, it's very uncomfortable."

Content with her job as a schoolteacher, and close with her sister and nephew, Clara was devastated when her son and husband decided to leave Russia. But Clara went, making the kind of sacrifice, in 1977, that seems part of an earlier, more heroic era. Clara is a modern version of all the millions of European Jews who pulled up roots before her—many not because they wanted to but because they had to.

There are compensations. "The freedom here is unbelievable," she says. "I cannot believe things you can say about Reagan." Clara notices that I'm left-handed. "No one," she says, "is allowed to be lefty in Russia."

Clara isn't kidding. Nor is she kidding when she talks about the censorship she faced as a literature teacher. It wasn't until she arrived in this country that she was able to read some of the greatest books her country has produced, among them Boris Pasternak's *Dr. Zhivago*. As Yakov puts it, "It's not just that she couldn't get it in the library. She didn't even know that it existed."

She has also found religious freedom. "Back in Russia," Clara says, "we were ashamed to say that we are Jewish." Incredibly, Yakov was fifteen before he learned he wasn't Christian—his parents hid the fact because they didn't want people to pick on him. "There was one synagogue in Odessa," Clara remembers, "but it was very far. Only the oldest, oldest people went. If I went to synagogue, in one minute I lose my job.

"Here, I like that people can go to synagogue. Once a year we go—on Yom Kippur." She has been to her first Passover seder, and she has seen her first bar mitzvah. "We never went to one in Russia. It was so exciting."

Clara was born in Odessa, in the days when that port city was more than half Jewish. She lived most of her life in one room—part of a communal apartment, with a single bathroom, that housed five families. Until recently, one of those families consisted of Clara, her mother, her husband, Naum, and Yakov, their only child. "I work, my husband works, my mother is sick, all in one room—how can you have more children?" asks Clara. "But now we're sorry that we didn't."

Only families with less than 6 square meters per person qualified to receive bigger apartments, Clara explains. And since her family shared 25 square meters (6 1/4 each), there was no chance of moving. Says Clara, "Yakov was born in that room. If we hadn't left he would have died there." The situation was particularly frustrating for Naum, an engineer who helped erect large buildings.

That's not all. "We have not car, and we have not telephone," says Clara. "My husband, for ten years, is in line for a telephone—and he is a veteran of the war."

In Russia, I had a convertible car: a bicycle. . . . We also played games. They say, "Pac-man," and you do . . . Russian TV is great. We had two channels. On one, you get the official version of the news. On the other, there's a KGB agent with a gun saying, "Turn back to Channel One." . . . But there are some better programs: *One Day to Live, Bowling for Food, Wonder Woman*—she looks like a woman, but you wonder. . . . Sure, I had designer jeans in Russia. Calvin Kremlins. If they could talk, they'd be shot. . . .

Says Clara, "We weren't poor, and we weren't rich. We had enough to live. We had a pretty good room compared to most people, and we made a curtain to divide it."

There is no Oil of Olay in Russia, but there is perfume: Evening in Prison. But it's understandable. When you look at a Russian woman's night table, you see that in daytime it's a stove. . . . Also, Russian women work harder than men. A man can spend eighteen hours behind the plow, but the woman is in front of it. . . .

She also tolerated her job, despite the fact that each year she was given new textbooks; often, they completely contradicted the previous year's lessons. What she was required to teach, she taught. Says Clara, "You do not question; you just accept. I liked the kids, and I liked to work. It's not like first we were free. We just knew what was needed."

Clara's views—which she now calls "naïve"—pitted her against Naum, a long-time critic of the Soviet system. Yakov remembers him sitting up nights listening to "Voice of America" broadcasts. It was Naum who first suggested emigration. But Yakov wanted to stay put. He was making a name for himself performing in local theaters and on a Black Sea cruise ship ("the love barge"). Then he began to feel the sting of censorship. Once a year, he was required to submit all his jokes to party censors, who deleted some of his best lines. What they left was it for the entire year. He couldn't add material or ad-lib.

What kind of jokes did the censors approve? "Anything that made the country look good," says Yakov. "They didn't care if it was funny." Once, Yakov said, they wouldn't let him use the word "red" in a joke about American Indians—and there was no substitute punch line.

Growing up in Russia, my father wanted me to be the same thing he was: a suspect. Here you have freedom of speech. You can go up to Reagan and say, "I don't like Ronald Reagan." In Russia you can do the same thing. You can go up to the party chief and say, "I don't like Ronald Reagan." We also had secret ballots in Russia. Secret from me. . . .

Yakov was also disturbed because, as a Jew, he was prevented from performing outside Russia. When his cruise ship headed toward Roumania, Yakov was rudely ordered to get off. Says his mother, "He was greatly . . ." She is looking in her dictionary. "He was greatly to be offended."

About the same time, Jews began leaving Russia in large numbers. Naum's sister moved to Israel, and other friends left for the States. They would write back and—in guarded language—urge Naum and Clara to follow.

Clara was opposed to the idea. In addition to her personal misgivings, she was convinced that Yakov wouldn't be able to work as a comedian in the United States, that "he'd be frustrated for the rest of his life."

There was a lot of fighting. Then Yakov took his mother on a Black Sea cruise to show her that he could make foreign audiences laugh. That's when she began to come around.

Before the family applied for exit visas, Clara retired, to avoid dismissal from her job. Yakov lost his job. But a sympathetic club owner let him work off the books as a dishwasher to keep the family from starving. Old friends, Yakov recalls, suddenly began calling him a "dirty Jew." More than two years passed. Then the family was told they had to leave the country in a few hours. The bags they were allowed to pack were thrown open and emptied on the railroad platform for the benefit of everyone who'd come to see them off. Says Yakov, "They wanted you to look disgraced for leaving."

> I got out of Russia in an unusual way: alive. They let me take out four things they didn't break—my arms and my legs. . . . They make things tough: interrogations, making you say things you don't want to —they use the same techniques that you use here on *60 Minutes*. . . .

"It was impossible to leave," recalls Clara, but she left. After a three-month layover in Rome, the family arrived in New York with less than five hundred dollars. Says Yakov, "At the airport, the immigration official asked me what I wanted to be. I said, 'A comedian.' He laughed. And I thought, 'I'm not doing bad already.' "

The first few months were the hardest for Clara, especially since Yakov insisted on living away from New York's Russian-Jewish community. His goal was to learn English quickly, and he did—mostly by watching TV. It was harder for Clara, who says, "I ask him, 'Talk to me one time in English.' But he has not the patience."

But she did learn Yiddish. Explains Clara, "A lot of Jewish people use a little English, a little Yiddish, and they think it's all English. Talking to them was a big mistake."

> I knew I had to learn your language to get a job. So I locked myself in a room for three months and watched TV. Then I found out it was a Spanish station. . . . At first, America confused me. I went into a restaurant, and they said, "How many in your party?" I said, "Two hundred million." . . . What do I like best about America? Warning shots. Oh, and Roach Motels. Only America would have motels for roaches. What a country. . . .

Naum and Clara made a few dollars assembling Christmas tree ornaments in their apartment in Washington Heights. Yakov moved to Florida, where he took up bartending and attended college. Says Clara, "It was very hard. Not money, not language, not Yakov."

Smirnoff's next stop was Grossinger's, the Catskills resort, where he signed on as a busboy. Says Clara, tearfully, "My husband and I were very, very shamed and we were sorry we had come. We thought, 'We didn't come all the way to America for him to be a busboy.' We were hoping for maybe computers, anything. In Russia, he finished refrigeration college. He's a good mechanic and a good engineer." She adds, "We with Yakov had a lot of fighting."

But Yakov stuck to his puns. Soon he was onstage at Grossinger's, and he was getting laughs. Within a year, he moved the family to Los Angeles—but for his parents, California proved even more isolating than New York. Naum, an inventor, worked on his devices for the handicapped and a door chain with a shock absorber over it (so it can't be cut). But he was unable to interest manufacturers in his products. According to Yakov, "My parents just sat home, and they were frustrated. I hated to see them like that."

Yakov solved the problem by buying his parents a dilapidated house in the Hollywood Hills. They plan to fix it up, then sell it. "I promised them the profits," says Yakov. "They're becoming capitalist pigs. When I got my last movie, my mother said, 'Good, now we can put in a pool.'"

Clara also made a little money of her own playing Yakov's mother in *Brewster's Millions*. But she has hardly gone Hollywood. "To me, he was funnier in Russian," Clara says. "The Russian jokes I understand. In English, I don't understand, and when he translates them, they don't sound funny."

Then she adds, "A lot of jokes, he doesn't want to translate. He knows we won't like them. They're probably about sex."

Clara would like to see Yakov marry—"if not a Russian Jewish girl then American Jewish." She says, "I want three children for Yakov. One is not enough. Two is okay, but three is better.

"That's what I want, but Yakov, I don't know."

Then Clara adds, "And I want them to believe in God. This God is in my heart. But I don't want them to be very religious. This is America in the twentieth century. I want to be American, not only Jewish."

Harvey Fierstein's mother

JACKIE FIERSTEIN

"MY MOTHER SAID, 'IS HARVEY GAY?' AND I SAID, 'I
DON'T KNOW, MA. I DON'T SLEEP WITH HIM.'"

In her two-bedroom apartment, in the Sheepshead Bay section
of Brooklyn, Jackie Fierstein is sitting down to breakfast—a
buttered onion roll, a boiled egg, and o.j.—when the phone
rings. In no time, Jackie is talking about her sons: Harvey, the
Tony Award–winning playwright *(Torch Song Trilogy, La Cage
aux Folles),* and Ronald, a lawyer who is spending more and
more of his time investing Harvey's money.

*You saw the show? Did you like it? Very good. How were the
seats? Good. Did it get a standing ovation? Yeah.*

Can you believe our little boy did that?

*No, Harvey wasn't there. He's involved with the third show
now. It's going to open in February. And another group is going
to open* La Cage *in Los Angeles. So he's very busy—they're
auditioning people. I really don't see too much of him.*

*I don't know. I don't know. You'll have to ask Ronald. Even
Harvey doesn't know. He says to Ronald, "Can I have an ac-
counting?" Ronald says, "Harvey, what do you want? What is
your heart's desire?" So he says, "I don't know. Sometimes, I go
into a store, and I think, 'Can I buy this? Can I buy that?'" So*

Ronald says, "Harvey, the sky is the limit. Go in and buy what you wish." So he's so cute—he went to the Fulton Street Mall, and he bought himself a pair of shoes. I said, "I don't believe it. You mean, I'm not going to see you in those stupid sneakers anymore?"

Sure, sure, when do you want to come? I don't care. You're not in my way.

Yeah, his picture is on the new Life *magazine. But if you've got* People *magazine, he's one of the twenty-five—the twenty-five most intriguing people. And, yeah, that's him, in* Vogue, *with the high hat. I want you to know that he had a picture in* Hustler. *Harvey said, "It's not such a nice magazine." I could have killed him. I said, "I had to spend five dollars for that stupid magazine." I couldn't even show it to my friends, because of what's on the back. So now I have to get it mounted.*

Listen, I have a gentleman here. He's trying to interview me. Yeah. No, don't be silly. I don't talk to you that often.

Okay, darling, be well.

It is, I learn by spending time with Jackie, a conversation she is called on to repeat at least a dozen times a day.

Five years ago, the repartee would have been very different. Harvey was just another starving playwright then—"and I mean starving," says Jackie. Recently widowed, she would look for excuses to stop by his basement apartment, in another part of Brooklyn. When she brought him food, she'd insist, "Your mother still doesn't know how to shop for one; you'll have to take some." And when she wasn't at his place, she'd worry.

Occasionally, Jackie would take the subway to Manhattan to see one of Harvey's plays. None of them seemed destined for Broadway. *The International Stud* followed a drag queen on a visit to a "backroom" bar, where he engaged in simulated intercourse with a virile stranger. *Fugue in a Nursery* explored the relationships between the same drag queen (named Arnold Beckoff), Arnold's lover, and the lover's wife.

"The first time I went, I just sat there," says Jackie. "A lot of these things I had never seen before. And there were questions in my mind; it's natural. But since my husband was already dead, I didn't have anyone I could ask. He was a very wise man and I was always the kind of person who, if we went somewhere and someone told a joke, my husband would have to explain it to me later.

"And I couldn't ask any of my friends," Jackie goes on, "because they were just as naïve as I was. So mostly I waited patiently in the theater until somebody discussed it, and then I listened. It was quite an education for me." If Harvey was uncomfortable about her being there, Jackie remembers, "he didn't say anything to me, and I didn't say anything to him."

Harvey's third play, *Widows and Children First* (which, with the other two, makes up his *Trilogy*), dealt in part with a somewhat more familiar subject: the relationship between a gay person (still the drag queen Arnold Beckoff) and his mother, a Jewish dynamo who arrives from Florida to try to straighten out his life:

MA: Arnold, do what you want. You want to live like this? Gay gezzintah hait. I don't care anymore. You're not going to make me sick like you did your father.

ARNOLD: I made my father sick?

MA: No; he was thrilled to have a fairy for a son! You took a lifetime of dreams and threw them back in his face.

ARNOLD: What lifetime of dreams? He knew I was gay for fourteen years.

MA: What? You think you walk into a room and say, "Hi Dad, I'm queer," and that's that? You think that's what we brought you into the world for? Believe me, if I'd known I wouldn't have bothered. God should tear out my tongue, I should talk to my child this way. Arnold, you're my son, you're a good person, a sensitive person with a heart, kennohorrah, like your father and I try to love you for that and forget this. But you won't let me. You've got to throw me on the ground and rub my face in it. You haven't spoken a sentence since I got here without the word "gay" in it.

ARNOLD: Because that's what I am.

MA: If that were all you could leave it in there [Points to bedroom] where it belongs; in private. No, you're obsessed by it. You're not happy unless everyone is talking about it. I don't know why you don't just wear a big sign and get it over with.

Harvey's plays are largely autobiographical, and it's natural to wonder how much of Mrs. Beckoff is Jackie, how much of the dialogue between Arnold and Mrs. Beckoff was first uttered in Sheepshead Bay.

Jackie has heard the question before, and she's quick to answer. "I don't mind if people think I'm Mrs. Beckoff, because she's very funny. But I never thought of myself as that character," she says. "I would see Estelle Getty [who played the part on Broadway] in Harvey's dressing room, and she'd say, 'Am I doing okay?' And I'd say, 'Why not? You're a mother.' "

There is one episode Jackie claims as her own: when Mrs. Beckoff talks about her husband's death, she says she took home his belongings in a paper bag. Says Jackie, "That really happened to me. My husband had a heart attack at work. By the time they called me from the office, he was dead."

Otherwise, she says, "The character is universal. In the theater, I hear people talking—and everyone sees their mother in it. A lot of people relate. You don't even have to be gay—every mother wants the same things, that her kids have a nice home, some means of livelihood."

Then again, Jackie sees more than a bit of her own mother in Mrs. Beckoff. Harvey's grandmother is ninety and living in a nursing home upstate. "For years," says Jackie, "I've been calling her 'the little actress.' If she doesn't get her way, she gets a phony heart attack. That's how she shows me. She's always known how to manipulate me very well."

Indeed, Jackie recalls, "My mother didn't believe in college for girls. So when I was sixteen, I had to quit school to go to work. And by the time I was nineteen, my mother was calling me an old maid." So Jackie, who was still sharing a bedroom with her younger brother, married Irving Fierstein. Ten years her senior, "he was like a father figure," she says. "I was naïve, and he was a man of the world. He came from the mountains—the Catskills—and in the mountains, young men got experienced very fast."

The marriage, which lasted thirty-three years, was a good one, according to Jackie. But, she says, "I went from my mother's house to my husband's house. I was always under someone's thumb. We would make decisions together—he would let me rant as much as I wanted, but when he opened his mouth, I would shut up." To make matters worse, "my mother came to visit for at least three months a year. So I always had someone telling me what to do."

Now, for the first time in her life, Jackie says, "I'm independent."

Five days a week, she works as a librarian—a career she began after going back to high school and college in her forties —at an intermediate school in Brooklyn. It's not an easy life; students are abusive and money to buy books is scarce. Jackie reports, "My mother says, 'How come Harvey doesn't take care of you? How come the millionaire's mother has to work?' And I say, 'Why should I stop working?' When you take from someone else, you may not have to do exactly what they want, but you at least have to listen to them. This way, I'm spending my own money, and I can spend it the way I want. My choices may not always be wise, but they're my choices."

Jackie goes on, "A lot of people say to me, 'Why don't you meet somebody?' I say, 'I don't know.' I hesitate. I really don't know if I want to tie myself down. Sometimes I say, 'Yes, I do,' and sometimes I say, 'No, I don't.' I don't know if I want to have to run home and prepare dinner. I like to cook—I like being a homemaker—but I've been introduced to another world, and I like this business of being free and doing what I want."

Jackie's liberation parallels Harvey's. He has become the most visible and outspoken homosexual in the country. On talk shows, he happily converses about his lovers and about his own stints as a drag queen. And no gay rights parade in New York would be complete now without Fierstein waving from an open car.

Jackie recognizes the similarity between her evolution and Harvey's; she tells him, "I don't want you to tell me what I should be; you do with your life what you want." But it will be a long time before Jackie rides with Harvey in that open car. If she has come to terms with Harvey's success, the urge that prompted that success is one she still doesn't completely understand. "Harvey says that there are people everywhere who are gay and I am starting to see that," she admits. But it is not her favorite subject. "People in the building are very polite," she says. "They never bring it up."

On one of her fourteen or fifteen visits to *Torch Song,* Jackie recalls, "I took my mother. And when it was over, she turned to me and said, 'Jackie, is Harvey gay?' And I said, 'I don't know, Ma. I don't sleep with him.'

"I feel being gay is a personal thing," she explains. "This is where Harvey and I differ. I think he's made his point, and I wish he would go on to something else."

She offers an analogy: "Being a widow, I come in contact with a lot of other widows. If they have male companions, that's their business. I don't know if I would go that route. I'm very straitlaced. But whatever I did in my bedroom, I wouldn't make it public."

Jackie won't say when she first realized Harvey was gay. But she remembers, "Even as a child, he was different. Ronald was interested in sports, but Harvey never was. He was very artistic; he had hands of gold."

She says, "We never expected him to become a writer. We —Irving and I—encouraged him to take art education. We figured as a teacher you get off at three o'clock, you have your summers and your weekends free. You can still do your art. But at least you know the dollars are coming in."

Harvey tried teaching—in Jackie's school. He lasted exactly one day before returning to the theater. Ronald, meanwhile, was a folksinger. "Irving used to say, 'What am I going to do with my two bums?' I mean, there was a one in a million chance of his making it. Who thinks their son will be the one in a million?"

Not Jackie Fierstein. "I used to be just Jackie Gilbert," she says. "Then I became Mrs. Irving Fierstein. Then, when the boys were growing up, I was Harvey and Ronald's mother. When I went to work, I was Mrs. Fierstein again. And now? And now I'm back to being Harvey's mother."

Does that bother her? "If somebody came up to you and said, 'I saw your son on TV,' wouldn't you be proud?" she says. "It's like something rubbed off on you.

"As a parent, you feel like maybe you gave something—maybe your genes are there. I don't know—I don't think I'm so talented. I know my husband was very talented. My mother is very talented.

"I look at it that we set a good example, and that's that."

"Gene Simmons' mother

FLORENCE

"AS LONG AS HE DOESN'T SMOKE OR TAKE DRUGS, I'M HAPPY."

In ten years as a reporter, I have interviewed hundreds of couples. But no two people, not Taylor and Burton at war, or Belushi and Aykroyd at play, have made me laugh, and cry, and think, as much as Gene Simmons, the rock star, and his mother.

Gene is an accomplished producer, manager, and actor. But he is best known as the lead singer of Kiss, the phenomenally successful rock band famous for its garish white makeup and monster costumes. For years, Simmons refused to appear in public without that makeup, although it took him as long as two hours to apply (he carried a cosmetics case loaded with more than forty tubes, brushes, and bottles). At concerts, Simmons breathed fire, belched smoke, and flashed his trademark: a tongue of absurdly long and menacing proportions. But Kiss is more than the sum of its gimmicks: its twenty heavy metal albums have together sold an incredible 65 million copies.

I had my first encounter with Gene Simmons in a fabulously rock-starrish apartment. Gene had constructed, from scratch, a penthouse on the roof of a Manhattan building, and now he was decorating the place with floor-to-ceiling mirrors and "Mesopotamian" columns. But after we had talked for a few minutes, he asked me to accompany him on a visit to his mother on Long Island. Downstairs, a stretch limo complete with bar and Betamax awaited us. Forty minutes later, the limo was in another world: outside the split-level home that belongs to Gene's mother, Florence.

"Isn't she gorgeous?" Before the limo has even stopped, Gene has leaped out and is hugging his mother on the driveway. In her foyer, Florence, a petite blonde with a Zsa Zsa Gabor accent, has hung a banner: WELCOME HOME, MY DARLING ONLY SON. Upstairs, Florence serves the kind of meal that kept Gene at 220 pounds through high school, including bagels and lox and all the trimmings. She chides Gene for starting his cheesecake before eating his sandwich ("The only thing that worries me is that he'll gain"). Then, when Gene flashes his trademark, Florence sighs, "I told him never to stick out his tongue. He didn't listen."

Otherwise, Florence has no complaints about her son. "As long as he doesn't smoke or take drugs," she says, "I'm happy." She calls Gene "Chaim," which is the Hebrew word for "life," and wears a photograph of him in full Kiss makeup in her locket.

The only records Florence owns are Gene's—except for a few discs she puts in front of them, "so if a burglar gets in, hopefully he'll see those first." Playing one recent Kiss album, she sings along, seemingly oblivious to the lyrics: "Lick it up, there's something sweet you can't buy with money; come on, lick it up, lick it up." "I think it has something to do with sex," Florence observes. Protecting her ears with cotton, she comes to all of Gene's New York-area concerts.

In one of the four bedrooms of her house, Florence has a small clock radio continuously tuned to New York's WNEW-FM. "I never turn it off, because I never know when they're going to play Kiss." When the band does come on, she turns it up so loud that her husband, Eli, "goes crazy." She has also filled more than a dozen scrapbooks with articles about Gene: "My friends send them to me. They know I'm crazy."

Florence has turned her home into an unofficial Kiss museum. Three downstairs rooms are packed with Kiss memorabilia, including letters in which fans promise slavelike devotion to Florence's son. There are also gold and platinum records, a complete wardrobe of black leather and metal spikes (Gene's stage clothes) and a sampling of the Kiss merchandise that has made him rich. But the most elaborate artifacts are the huge needlepoints of a firebreathing Gene done by his mother. One, which took her three years to complete, bears the legend: "To my darling only son, who's the greatest star of rock and roll in the whole world." Says Florence, "I want to be able to look around the house and think of Chaim. It's a wonderful feeling having such a good person for a son."

She is equally loyal to Gene's friends. At first, Florence confused his longtime flame, Diana Ross, with Donna Summer. But now she says, "Diana has been a real good friend to Gene. It's hard, in his business, to have any real friends, because people are jealous." One year, Gene brought Diana and her ex-husband, Bob Silberstein, to Florence's house for a Passover seder. At another seder, Gene's guests were Cher, her daughter Chastity, and her son Elijah Blue. "I said, 'Gene, you're bringing Cher? She's such a fancy, schmancy lady.' And Gene said, 'No, she's just an ordinary, nice person.' And Gene was right." The seder guests, who included Gene's chauffeur ("I always invite him in. What's another plate?"), all put on yarmulkes, and Simmons led the service.

For her devotion, Florence claims she is amply rewarded. Gene phones her every week, "no matter where he is, even Japan." Of course, Florence calls him every day, and if his answering machine picks up, she talks for up to half an hour. "I just go blab, blab, blab," she says. "It's important for children, no matter how old they are, to know there's somebody who cares. Even when you're famous, you can still be lonely."

Does she overdo it? "My family thinks so," shrugs Florence, "but I'm not ashamed. He is my life. I don't have any other children. And his father wasn't here. We made it on our own—just me and Chaim."

Florence's concern for Gene is the happy result of a life filled with almost unbearable hardship. She is a survivor of the Holocaust, a subject she is not afraid to face. "Even when Chaim was little," she says, "if there was a TV show about it, I let him watch. Our children have to know what happened."

Born in Jund, Hungary, in the twenties, Florence worked in her parents' general store while apprenticing to a beautician.

But the Nazis interrupted her training, moving her first to a Jewish ghetto, in 1942, and then to Ravensbrück, the first of three concentration camps in which she managed to outlast the war. She survived only because the commandants' wives needed beauticians. Still, when the camps were liberated, Florence was near starvation. And she was just hours away from being gassed by the Nazis "so the Americans wouldn't find us."

The next two years were hardly better. She returned home to Hungary to find that her parents were dead and that strangers had taken over their house. She found solace in a Zionist youth group, where she met Gene's father. "He was the best-looking guy, and he said I was the best-looking girl." They married three months later, which, Florence says, was a mistake. "You need to know a person better."

The couple moved to Palestine, risking arrest by violating the British blockade. Gene's father went into the army; Florence was exempted because she was already pregnant. Life in Israel, she recalls, "was incredibly hard. There was no money to buy things. I made Gene's first winter coat from an army blanket."

When Gene was six, Florence divorced his father and followed her two brothers to New York. She found a job in a dress factory in Brooklyn, sewing buttons and buttonholes for "very little money." Her workday, including commuting, stretched from 6:30 A.M. to 9:30 P.M. "I was never home," she says. "It's lucky Gene went straight."

When he wasn't studying at Yeshiva, Gene kept busy. By the time he was in high school, he had learned enough English (on top of his Hebrew and Hungarian) to sell his own mimeographed science fiction magazine, typed on a typewriter Florence had shlepped home on the subway.

She also shlepped home a guitar. Soon Gene had formed his first rock group, the Long Island Sounds, and was a hit at weddings and bar mitzvahs. But he fulfilled a promise to Florence to finish college. When he graduated, Florence wanted him to be a teacher. So he tried teaching. But, Gene jokes, "no matter how good I was, the kids never applauded."

Gene begged Florence to let him become a professional

musician, and she relented. With high school chum Stanley Eisen (later Paul Stanley), Gene created Kiss, working as an office temp (or, as his mother puts it, a "Friday girl") to support himself until the band began attracting a following at concerts.

Soon the money was rolling in. Florence had trouble recognizing Gene in costume. Showing her a picture of the group, "Gene asked me if I knew which one was him. I said, 'Sure,' and I pointed to Stanley."

But the fans recognized Gene, and soon crowds were gathering outside Florence's house. "They would not believe Gene wasn't home," she says. "They would throw rocks at the windows, hoping he'd come out." Eventually, Gene bought her a place in a quieter neighborhood, where no one knew that Florence was a rock star's mother until her photograph appeared in *People.*

Now the neighbors know, but Florence doesn't let them treat her like a celebrity's mother. "When people act like I'm special," she says, "I say, 'I'm not the one. My son's the one.' The pleasure is all mine, but the credit is Chaim's."

Fran Lebowitz's mother

RUTH LEBOWITZ

"IF YOU'RE LOOKING FOR WAYS IN WHICH THE PAR-
ENTS INSPIRED HER, THERE AREN'T ANY. BUT I
HOPED A LOT."

The Washington *Post* has called her "the funniest woman in
America." Fran Lebowitz likes the Washington *Post*. Here are
some things she doesn't like: dogs, children, the rich, the poor,
algebra, sportscasters, the early nineteenth century, airlines,
Los Angeles, and brunch. She said so in dozens of "I Cover the
Waterfront" columns for Andy Warhol's *Interview*, and again in
two volumes of essays, *Metropolitan Life* and *Social Studies*,
which—from the top of the New York *Times* best-seller list—
confirmed her place as pop culture's preeminent wet blanket.
She is the favorite author of every Fred and Ethel Weltschmerz,
the cynic qua non of Manhattan's (and the Hamptons') ennui-
and-upward generation. And she is funny!

Twenty miles away, Ruth Lebowitz is Morristown, New
Jersey's reigning cynic's mother. Fran once told the New York
Times, "When I rang up my mother after the reviews [of *Metropolitan Life*] came out, she was too busy to get on the line. My
father told me she was giving out her latest interview to the
Morristown *Daily Record*. She started with me at the age of four
months, and, after a half-hour of talking, I was still only six."

When I read that, I knew Ruth Lebowitz was somebody I
had to meet. I called Fran—carefully waiting until after 3 P.M.
(the hour, according to *Metropolitan Life*, when the author

chooses to get out of bed). Fran told me to phone Tiger Lily, a clothing store for large women that Ruth Lebowitz owns with a couple of partners. I did, and Mrs. L. agreed to see me. A few days later, in a blinding snowstorm, I followed Mr. L.'s directions to their house. Ruth greeted me at the door, took my coat, then ushered me into the kitchen, where we stationed ourselves under a cow silkscreen signed by Andy Warhol.

Ruth Lebowitz: I'm very fond of the cow.

Fred Bernstein: I know Andy is one of Fran's best friends. What do you think of him?

RL: I know everything they write about him. All I know is, he's been very good to Francie.

FB: Do you always call her Francie?

RL: Yes. She was named for my husband's grandmother, who was Fanny. Frances was the best I could do. But once she moved to New York, she became Fran.

FB: Did you want her to be a writer?

RL: No, because we didn't know any writers. We didn't know any publishers. My husband had a furniture store, so there was no way we could help her. We knew she wanted to be a writer, but it seemed like an impossible thing.

FB: What did you want her to be?

RL: A teacher. I always believed being a schoolteacher was a good thing, because you have the same hours, the same vacations as your children. My mother thought the same thing, but I never did it either.

FB: So her interest in writing didn't come from you?

RL: No way. I use the phone. So if you're looking for ways in which the parents inspired her, there aren't any. But I hoped a lot that she would make it.

FB: So what's it like having a famous daughter?

RL: I would recommend it to anyone. I still go to work, I still do the laundry, I still do the cooking. But I do things I never would have done. It's added many nice things.

Ruth places a tray of coffee and cake in front of the cow.

FB: This is wonderful cherry strudel. Where did you get it?

RL: I baked it myself.

FB: Oh, really? You should write a cookbook.

RL: Liz Smith said that in her column. Every Christmas, I send her a batch of strudel. But I don't think I ever will. I'd rather be selling dresses.

FB: That reminds me. I expected you to be fat.

RL: Oh, yes, people always say that. But the last time I had a weight problem was during my freshman year in college. When I came home, my mother took one look at me, screamed, and put me on a diet.

FB: So how did you get into the large-size business?

RL: I went to see about decorating the store, and I got so enthusiastic. There are more and more good things being made for large women. It used to be that you could get a polyester dress, but you couldn't get a good wool suit. Besides, it's fun to have a new career after so many years of doing the same thing.

FB: You were a decorator?

RL: Yes, for twenty years.

FB: This house is gorgeous. But I can't believe Fran Lebowitz grew up here. What ever happened to the writer struggling to come up out of the ghetto?

RL: My grandfather came up out of the ghetto, and we're not going back.

FB: So it wasn't poverty that motivated her. How do you think you contributed to Fran's success?

RL: I haven't the faintest idea. If I'm going to be truthful, I have to admit she did it all herself. She wrote all the time, even when she was little. She never wanted to do anything else. She never wanted to be a stewardess or a nurse. I remember when my parents had their thirty-fifth anniversary at my sister's house, Francie wrote a play, all in rhyme, recounting the lives of my mother and father. I think she was nine.

FB: I'd love to see that play.

RL: I have a cousin in Georgia who kept a copy, and now she won't give it back.

FB: What was Fran like to raise?

RL: She was stubborn; she did whatever she wanted to do. She had a strong will and we couldn't change that.

FB: She often talks about getting kicked out of high school. What went wrong?

RL: She lost interest. If she thought an assignment was silly, she wouldn't do it. She's the kind of person who wants to do what she wants to do. Of course, we wanted her to go to college.

FB: Why?

RL: Because you want your kids to go to college.

FB: But Francie—now I'm calling her Francie—didn't want to?

RL: She said, "No way. A writer doesn't learn to write by taking a course in fourteenth-century French poetry. You learn to write by writing."

FB: Were you very disappointed?

RL: Let's put it this way: Francie says when she wins the Pulitzer Prize, I'll be sitting there crying. They'll say, "Look, your mother's crying because she's so happy," and Francie'll say, "No, she's crying because I never went to college." It was a constant source of friction for us.

FB: Instead of going to college, what did she do?

RL: She moved to New York, where she lived in a terrible place —it made us sick to go there. It really was not what we had in mind for our children.

FB: Did she complain?

RL: Never. We complained a lot.

FB: What did she do for money?

RL: She sold belts on the street. She drove for a guy who managed rock stars. Our one stipulation when she went to New York was that she had to take courses at the New School. And she did —until she got her first job with Andy Warhol. She used to work for them as a gofer and on the phone, trying to get advertising, which she would be the first to admit she's not too good at. Then someone at *Interview* asked her to write movie reviews. She couldn't live on what they paid, so then we did help her with money.

FB: Then what?

RL: Then an editor at Dutton called . . .

FB: And the rest is history.

RL: When *Metropolitan Life* came out, Andy gave her a big party at Regine's. We were in a coffee shop across the street, watching the limousines pull up, and I said to Harold, "What if she had listened to us?" I don't mean that having a famous kid makes your life marvelous—but it's an added little thing. It's fun to go into a restaurant and have the headwaiter run over and have people recognize her. I'm human—I get a big charge out of that.

FB: What do people say about her books?

RL: What they say—to me—is that they're wonderful. Both books were best-sellers in Morristown. The day *Metropolitan Life* was reviewed in the New York *Times*, my phone rang at seven A.M. It was my friend Elsie. She had just gotten her paper, and it was a rave.

FB: Are you bothered by the reviews that aren't raves?

RL: Once I was at the hairdresser reading *People* magazine, and it said *Social Studies* was a bad book. It was the first time I'd read a negative review. My hair stood right up on end. On the other hand, it's amazing that as many people liked the book as did. I really don't know how it became a best-seller in the Midwest.

FB: Is the Fran Lebowitz of *Social Studies* the same Fran Lebowitz who grew up in this house?

RL: Well, she exaggerated a little for the book, but basically those are her attitudes. She is very perceptive. She sees through everything.

FB: Does that ever cause problems?

RL: Well, I have a friend whose son is incensed with her because she wrote that people in New York should not be allowed to have dogs. He went off on this whole thing at dinner. I thought it was stupid, but what can you say? She does not like animals. Also, she gets anti-Semitic mail. That doesn't surprise me. I think anti-Semitism is a fact of life. But I get a little scared. She does a lot of college lecturing—she walked into one auditorium, and somebody had hung a swastika up. Of course, she's very visible. She never changed her name. She did a benefit for the Jewish Center—she raised money for the Sisterhood.

FB: She sounds very down-to-earth. Has making lots of money changed her?

RL: She got a big apartment—that was her one extravagance. She didn't go out and buy a mink coat. She's not that interested in clothes. She would be happy living her life in a pair of jeans. But for her sister's wedding, she really came through. She had a beautiful outfit made in white satin.

FB: So you're saying that she hasn't changed much?

RL: Sometimes, people get very alienated from their families when they move on to a different level. But that hasn't happened. She is truly the most loving kind of person. She comes to every family thing, every wedding, every bar mitzvah. And she never comes out here that she doesn't get in the car and visit my father in the nursing home. She brings him things he can't get out here—a tongue sandwich.

FB: How did he react to the book?

RL: To my father, that his granddaughter had written a book was the greatest thing that ever happened to him. When *Metropolitan Life* came out, he kept it in his lap for I think four months.

FB: How much of a Jewish background do you have?

RL: I grew up in a kosher home in Derby, Connecticut. My grandfather, who lived in Bridgeport, had trained to be a rabbi in Russia. But my great-grandfather was already a rabbi in Bridgeport, and they didn't need two rabbis. That left my grandfather with no real skills to make a living. So my father, who was the oldest son, left school in the sixth grade to help support the family.

FB: Derby, Connecticut, sounds like a pretty cloistered environment.

RL: I wasn't totally sheltered. During the Holocaust, we had refugees come stay with us until they found places to live. One, Dr. Barron, had hands that were all deformed. He said the Nazis had broken his fingers one by one and hadn't set them.

FB: Do you think of yourself as a Jewish mother?

RL: Definitely. Being a Jewish mother is not such a terrible thing. I had a Jewish mother, and she was fine.

FB: Would you like to see Fran get married?

RL: Well, she's very self-sufficient. I don't think she needs it in her life. Of course, I'd love to make that wedding.

With another piece of strudel for fortification, I prepare to go off into the blizzard. Mrs. Lebowitz is worried that I won't make it home safely.

RL: I'll tell you what I tell my kids. Call me collect when you get there, and ask for yourself.

❧Harry Reems' ❧
mother

RAZIE STREICHER

"No matter what you do, you might as well do
it the best."

Like a lot of women in Miami Beach, Razie Streicher likes to
show people she meets photographs of her children. Her youngest is named Herbie. "When people see him," Razie says,
"they usually say, 'Gee, your Herbie looks familiar, but I don't
know why.' Most of the time, I figure it's because they saw him
in the movie."

The movie in question is *Deep Throat,* and it's no wonder
people can't quite place the face. Herbie—who goes by the
name Harry Reems—plays a libidinous sex therapist, a sort of
Dr. Verystrangelove, and it's not his face that fills the screen.
Harry got paid a hundred dollars for his vigorous performance,
which took less than a day to film. *Deep Throat* went on to
become the biggest-grossing porno movie of all time, earning its
producers, roughly, $25 million. Released in 1972, it's still making them money.

Razie, a soft-spoken, sixty-five-year-old widow, has never
seen *Deep Throat.* She says, "I can guess what it's about from the
title. But I have no interest in going, and I don't think Herbie
would want me to go."

Not that she's ashamed to talk about the movie. When the
other women in her Collins Avenue apartment building brag
about "my son the doctor" or "my son the lawyer," Razie
chimes in with "my son the porn star." She explains, "When

they ask, I'll say he's Harry Reems. And sometimes, I'll tell them
even if they don't ask. I always tell the truth. No one has ever
said a bad word: maybe they're too flabbergasted." Anyway,
Razie may just be staving off future embarrassments: "You
know how these things get around.

"When it first came out," Razie continues, "it was like *A
Star Is Born.* All my friends were calling me. They stood on line
to see it. They told me he was very cute and funny. Maybe they
said other things, I don't know, but not to me.

"At first, I was very upset," she admits. "But there was
nothing I could do. You have to grin and bear it. It's his life, not
mine. But now it doesn't bother me. I guess you mellow with
age.

"He's different from other celebrities," she muses. "But I
guess no matter what you do, you might as well do it the best."

A painting of Harry's father, Danny, who died in 1966,
hangs prominently over Razie's sofa. "What would he have
thought of Harry's movies?" I ask her, inadvertently eliciting
the whole story of how Herbert Streicher became Harry
Reems.

"I don't figure Herbie would have done it if my husband
had lived," says Razie. "He never would have done it, never.

"He couldn't accept my husband's death.

"You see, Danny had lung cancer. He had an operation, but
he went back to work, he played his golf.

"Even I didn't know how bad it was, until our twenty-fifth
wedding anniversary. We had a big party, and then we stayed
over in a hotel. I was unpacking Danny's bags when I found the
painkillers. That's how I knew.

"But I kept it from the children for a long, long time. Even
from Herbie, and he lived at home. He was eighteen. I didn't
want him to know. But he finally found out from one of his
friends—the friend's mother was my closest friend, and he must
have heard her talking to me about it.

"Herbie was devastated. I don't think he wanted to face it.
He became like a lost soul. He just bummed around. And then
he joined the Marines. He had started college that summer, but

before he'd even finished a year, he enlisted. Of course, I was upset—this was during Vietnam. But Danny says, 'If he wants to go, he goes.' I don't think Herbie could take living at home.

"When Danny died, Herbie made an appeal to get out of the service, so he could help me run his father's printing business. It was denied, and he was about to be shipped out to Vietnam. Then, at a club, he met a colonel who had been in exactly the same situation years before, and he helped him get an honorable discharge.

"So Herbie came to New York to help me run the business. But we had terrible difficulties. He thought he should make more money, that he wasn't compensated enough.

"Then a friend of his brought over a Swedish girlfriend, but she couldn't stay at his house. So Herbie asked if she could stay with us. I said, 'Okay, for a while.' So she moved in, and pretty soon she and Herbie were shacking up—in my house. And it was more than a while. She wasn't leaving. So I made her go, and he went with her. They were living in a hotel someplace.

"It was like a horror story. Then she had a fight with him, and he didn't have any money. That's when he got into the pornos, right at that time.

"It was a classic situation. Herbie was working in the crew of a porno film, doing lighting, and the leading man couldn't go on. Herbie jumped into the situation."

"Harry" went home with a hundred dollars but never made another penny from the film. "Can you imagine, for something like that, not getting royalties?" says Razie. "If you're going to do it, you might as well make a few bucks."

Then, in 1974, Harry was charged by an ambitious Tennessee prosecutor with "conspiring to import obscene material across state lines." Ironically, Harry had never even been to Tennessee before the trial, which lasted nine grueling weeks. "I felt so sorry for him," says Razie. "I used to call him every day. I said, 'Should I come?' and he said, 'No, Ma. Stay where you are.' I guess he didn't want me to get too upset."

The jury took only fifteen minutes to convict him. "It was so unfair," says Harry's mother. "I mean, he had nothing to do with importing the film. He just starred in it. Linda Lovelace was in it too—why didn't they get her? They needed someone to pick on, so they picked on Herb. It wasted so much money."

His appeal was paid for, in part, by such celebrities as Shirley MacLaine, Warren Beatty, Barbra Streisand, Jack Nicholson, and Ryan O'Neal, who understood the case's First Amendment implications. So did Harvard constitutional law expert Alan Dershowitz, who ultimately won a reversal of Harry's conviction. "When that happened," says Razie, "I was the happiest person in the world."

In the end, the publicity helped him. After *Throat*, Harry starred in *The Devil in Miss Jones* and more than a dozen other films. "He was sought after," says Razie. "He was a box office attraction."

Eventually, Harry tried acting (off-off Broadway) and, more recently, producing documentaries for cable. But at thirty-seven he began starring in porno films again. "I just talked to him last night, and that's what he told me," says Razie. "I said, 'Do what you think is best. But you're not getting any younger. I don't know how you do it.' "

I ask Razie to tell me about herself.

"Well, there's nothing much to tell, really," she says. "I never went to college."

"Go on," I say.

"The reason I never went is that the summer before I graduated high school, I worked as a model. And I made a lot of money. And to tell you the truth, I much preferred the money."

She was born Razel Steinberg. Actually, Razel is her Yiddish name, but, she says, "After all these years, if anyone called me Rose, I wouldn't turn around."

She was brought up in the Bronx, where her father was a well-to-do milliner and her mother "a typical hausfrau." She met her husband when she was only fifteen, but didn't marry him till six years later. In the meantime, she "kept company with a lot of different boys. I guess I was looking for something better. But Danny was always there waiting for me to come back. It was on again, off again, on, off, on, off. Finally, I told him, 'Let's get married.' "

She soon realized, "He was the most wonderful man. Everybody loved him." He was also a successful businessman, and the family lived in a large house in Harrison, New York. Razie kept kosher—"otherwise, my mother couldn't eat there."

She raised three children—Herbie, Rosalind, and Bob. "Herbie had a load of friends—they were always in our house. And he was hardworking. He always looked for a way to make a buck. He shoveled driveways, he caddied."

But he was also the mischievous one. "Once, we had just bought a new Cadillac. And we went out to the garage, and Herbie, who was four, had taken a can of paint and painted the Cadillac. Danny just laughed and laughed and laughed. I mean, it was funny, but I didn't think it was that funny. Danny was a very easygoing guy.

"He'll be dead eighteen years this Labor Day," Razie goes on. "Everybody loved Danny. To pack Riverside [funeral home] on a Labor Day—that's really something, right?"

After his death, and after her ill-fated attempt to run the business, Razie retired to Florida. Because she suffers from emphysema, Razie says, "I needed to get to a warm climate. It was here or Arizona, and my brother and sister were here."

She tried to enjoy her leisure. She dated two men. "Once and once. But I didn't want to get married." These days, illness keeps her in. So she does volunteer work at home, writing letters for the Women's Cancer League. She reads: "I go through books, and then I give them to the veterans." And she watches TV sports: "The Olympics were the best two weeks of my life."

Sometimes, flipping through the cable guide, she'll see a listing for "Harry Reems in *Deep Throat.*" But if she wants to see her son, she needn't look past her living room wall. "He's really so cute," she says, admiring a row of photographs of Herbie.

"He would have made a good doctor or lawyer," Razie muses. "But mostly, I just wanted him to be a good boy. And he is. I really think he is."

Melissa Manchester's mother

RUTH MANCHESTER

"As different as our household was, Melissa was more different."

"I was born a crazy kid into a crazy life with crazy parents who exposed me to wonderful things," says Melissa Manchester, recalling her childhood on the Upper West Side of Manhattan. But to her parents, David, a bassoonist, and Ruth, a painter turned clothing designer, the craziest thing is that their daughter is a star.

The New York *Times* has called Melissa Manchester "a singer at the peak of her craft," and millions of fans agree. Her twelve albums have produced almost that many hits, including "Don't Cry Out Loud" and "Whenever I Call You Friend." Most were written by Melissa—and if that's not enough, she has also composed hits for Johnny Mathis, Aretha Franklin, and others.

Melissa is a star, and she has the house to prove it: a sprawling, ultra-modern Hollywood Hills ranch, with a pool and an expansive view of L.A., which she shares with Kevin De Remer, her husband since 1982. (She was divorced from Larry Brezner, her former manager, in 1980.) Here, Melissa entertains such friends as Burt Bacharach, Carole Bayer Sager, Kenny Loggins, and Barry Manilow (who launched her career by getting her a job as one of Bette Midler's original backup singers, the Harlettes).

But the bright-eyed, red-haired woman who greets me at the door of the Hollywood Hills home isn't Melissa. It's Melissa's mother, Ruth, who's house-sitting while "my Meliss" is on the road. Ruth takes me on a tour of the house, stopping to stir the beef stew on the stove, and then, over coffee and cake, we talk.

So, what's it like having a famous daughter?

In New York, I was Ruth Manchester. Now everyone knows me as Melissa's mother. But it gets you great tables in restaurants, let me tell you.

You look so much like her. Even your mannerisms are the same.

Thanks. But she's been watching me a lot longer than I've been watching her.

Did you ever want to be a performer yourself?

Oh, for about two minutes. Then I had to go to work. My theory is that I would have if I had wanted to badly enough.

Was it your dream for Melissa to be famous?

It wasn't my dream. It was her dream. Singing is all she ever wanted to do. She was very single-minded. We could always see that she knew where she was going.

When did you first realize she had talent?

Even as a baby we knew she was special. We knew from the day she was born.

How could you tell?

You have to understand our household—there was always music. David, my husband, is a bassoonist—you make reeds, you practice. You'd play "Greensleeves," and she'd go twirling around. And you would always hear her singing.

Did that make her a fun kid to have around?

Well, sometimes she was a pain in the ass. As different as our household was, Melissa was more different.

How was she in school?

A daydreamer. She fantasized a lot. The teachers would call me in to talk about her. I'd say, "Whatever you're saying is probably true, but it doesn't matter." Because she knew what she wanted to do.

How did she get her start in music?

When she was about three, we bought her a dollar ninety-eight clarinet for Christmas. There were a lot of other presents, but that was the only one she noticed.

You celebrated Christmas?

Well, we exchanged presents. But there was no tree—my mother would have killed me. On Hanukkah, we'd light the candles and have latkes. I still light candles every Friday night. Usually, I go out, but first I light the candles.

Did she like taking piano lessons?

I don't care if she enjoyed them or not. Music has nothing to do with whether you like it.

You're kidding.

Of course I'm kidding. We found a teacher who was great. Except, for five years, he didn't know that she couldn't read music. Then he figured it out—that she was playing things from memory, after hearing them once. He wrote us a letter. That's when we realized she had this incredible gift.

Did other people see it?

People knew. You just saw this thing walk into a room and you knew. She's very quiet; she didn't have to talk.

How did she get started in the business?

Steven Cagan, her brother-in-law, was composing and producing jingles. One day, when she was about fourteen, he said, "You want to make some money? Come downtown." She did a lot of commercials for Steven. She was out of school half the time.

[The phone rings; Ruth tells her friend she'll call her back.]

Go ahead, talk for a few minutes.

This is not a few-minute friend; this is a half-hour friend.

We were talking about Melissa. What's it like for her, being a star?

I hate to dispel the truth, but it isn't very glamorous. Mostly, it's hard work. Melissa's always working. And when she's not working, she's thinking about working.

Does she work too hard?

Maybe, but from the parent's point of view, I understand. It's hard to be great unless you keep at it. When it's your kid, you're always worried. Every time she does something, you think, "Can she sustain that level?"

Does she?

Always. Every performance is thrilling. I've never seen her give a bad performance.

Do you think of her as "My daughter, the star"?

No way. She's still the Melissa who calls and says, "Ma, what are you cooking tonight?" That's your life—the other's not your life. People think you have butlers and maids. But it's just us. She makes the bed in the morning.

What are the disadvantages of having a famous daughter?

Well, I worry. There are a lot of crazy folks out there. I get scared out of my mind when she performs outdoors. I find it very unsettling. That's the other side of fame.

Has anything frightening ever happened to you?

Only that I get calls in the middle of the night, saying, "Are you Melissa's mother?" I say, "Yes." What am I supposed to say? Anyway, I guess it's sweet that they go to all the trouble to find me.

Did you worry about her after the divorce?

Yes, when we would drop her off alone in this house, I was berserk. Talk about unhappy.

But now she's remarried.

Kevin is one of those kind, gentle people. They have a lovely life.

What made you come out to L.A.?

The feeling that one shouldn't be separated from one's children, ever—at least not me and my children.

How did the move come about?

Well, Melissa called me in New York one day when she was working out here, and she said, "Ma, I bought a house." I said, "You want me to say I'm happy? Well, I'm not happy."

Your other daughter lives here too?

Yes. Claudia and Steven came out on July 4, 1976. Steven calls it his Independence Day. David said, "I think it's great." But I cried for two years.

So what happened?

Claudia and Melissa started calling and saying, "You've got to move out." Then my sons-in-law started calling and saying, "You've got to come; the girls are miserable." I said to David, "I'm gonna die unless we move out there." So we did.

But you had careers.

David was playing with the Metropolitan Opera. I had had a very good clothing business, but I closed it. It was too hard to do—imports, unions, and all kinds of silly things.

What do you do now?

I tried "going to lunch," but I got so bored. I have to know this is what I've got to do today. So now Claudia has a clothing business. It's called Kingsbridge Road—that's where we lived in the Bronx when the girls were little. I design the clothes. All of us are creative; it's such a special present.

What's your husband doing now?

David is helping to form a small opera company in Ventura. And he plays golf. And he plays concerts; he played in the opening and closing of the Olympics.

What's he like?

He's a great husband and a great guy. He was my childhood sweetheart back in the Bronx. I married young—it's been forty-three years in August. I don't know where it went.

What was it like when he was playing at the Met?

Terrific. People said, "How can you be married to a man who works every night?" But he was always home when the kids got home from school.

You've come a long way from the Bronx. What was your childhood like?

My parents came here from a small town near Kiev. My father had TB, so my mother brought three of us up, working in a garment factory as a finisher. It was terrible. You don't dwell on it.

But I'm interested.

You want to hear about it? You want to hear about half a chicken for five people? My mother had to kill herself to keep us in high school. She was a rock—and pretty. She was so pretty. Her name was Jenny Polsky.

How did you deal with poverty?

I fantasized a lot—we had nothing to eat, and I was designing evening gowns in my mind. But really, I learned very hard lessons.

Like what?

Like, with my background, there was no way I was ever going to be poor again. Just no way. Still, when I look around, I can't believe I have it so good.

What's been the best part?

When Melissa was little, I used to take her to Radio City to see the Rockettes. So when she performed there, David and I were beside ourselves. Can you imagine? As many times as I've seen her perform, I had to say, "Is that our kid? Is that Meliss? Our Meliss?"

❧ Marvin Mitchelson's ❧ mother

SONIA MITCHELSON

"MY LOSSES WERE HARSH AND HEAVY. . . . NEVER-
THELESS, MY GAINS WERE CONSIDERABLE. . . . I
ADMIT HUMBLY THAT MY BALANCE SHEET IS
FAIR."

Marvin Mitchelson made headlines in 1979, when he went to court on behalf of Michelle Triola, Lee Marvin's former girl-friend—and in the process invented the concept of "palimony." He has also played the game of high-stakes Hollywood divorce for Bianca Jagger, Pamela Mason, Anna Kashfi (Marlon Brando's ex), Zsa Zsa Gabor, and Connie Stevens—and, because it takes two to untangle, Richard Harris, Tony Curtis, Sonny Bono, Carl Sagan, and Mel Tormé. These days, Mitchelson has more stars on his client roster than a red-hot William Morris agent.

Not surprisingly, Marvin's book, *Made in Heaven, Settled in Court*, has become the unofficial bible of the breakup, and he has appeared on the cover of *People*, an honor usually reserved for the celebrities he counsels. But all of that's just gravy. His fees range up to $500,000 per case.

Still, I believe Marvin's mother, Sonia, should have been the lawyer in the family. The minute I arrived at her Los Ange-les apartment, Sonia began handing me documents. From drawers filled with neatly Xeroxed copies of what seemed like every letter she has ever written or received, Sonia Mitchelson, just like a lawyer, produced a pile of papers I was certain I would have no use for.

But when I started to read, I realized the letters Sonia had given me were far from boring. In fact, they captivated me; they made me think and, at times, cry. If she had ever been asked to prove in court that Jewish mothers are the most compassionate creatures on earth, Sonia Mitchelson would have won the case hands down. Here are some of Sonia's papers:

Exhibit A

[On her eightieth birthday, in 1982, Marvin had published, in a limited edition, Sonia's memoirs, which she had written at his sisters' urging. Sonia tells the story of Jacob Knoppow, her paternal grandfather, who moved from Pereyaslav, in the Ukraine, to Detroit, Michigan, in 1866. But Jacob, unhappy in the Promised Land, returned home two years later. In 1911, Jacob's son Simon (Sonia's father) faced the unhappy prospect of supporting a wife and five children in the Ukraine, where, according to Sonia, "many trades and occupations were prohibited to Jews, and higher education, with a few exceptions, was not allowed to Jewish children." So Simon Knoppow retraced his father's steps. He moved to Detroit, went into the paint and wallpaper business, and six months later sent for his wife and children. Sonia picks up the story.]

After Father sent us the necessary papers and money for the trip to the U.S.A., and after we sold our furniture and all our household goods, we found to our dismay that my brother Isaac's birth was not recorded, so he could not leave Russia. By the time this was corrected, World War I had broken out. All trips were canceled. We found ourselves without household goods, with very little money, and cut off entirely from Father's support.

Though Mother's sisters helped us with some furniture, the drastic change in our expectations was too much for my delicate mother. She suffered a stroke that took her to the hospital, then began a prolonged recovery at home. Thus I found myself, at the tender age of eleven, head of an impoverished household, with an ill mother to care for and with six mouths to feed.

Those were indeed harsh days. I learned in a hurry to wash laundry, to carry water from the river peasant-style—two pails on a contraption placed on the shoulders, which in itself was no small task—and to saw and cut the wood for the stove where I cooked, baked, and where we all warmed ourselves. There was no electricity. . . .

Mother was slowly improving. I tried my best to see to her needs first, at times even shortchanging myself if there was not enough to go around. My aunts helped as much as they could, but they themselves came upon very hard times. They lost all five of their sons in the war.

When things got desperate for us, Grandfather Jacob invited us to live with him. We made the necessary adjustments, joined Grandfather's synagogue, and settled in with the hope that the war would be over soon and that we would be on our way to the U.S.A. But the war raged on. The whole of Russia suffered hunger and privation—the Jews the most.

Two years after our coming, Grandfather took ill and died. Basheva [Sonia's step-grandmother] followed him within several months. Their last illnesses and the funeral expenses exhausted our material possessions. We found ourselves in another dire situation, without any relatives, completely on our own in a strange city. Abe [one of Sonia's brothers] was apprenticed to a tailor, a man Grandfather knew. Abe got his board but came home nights. Nathan [another brother] was apprenticed to a boot-maker; he, too, got his board and came home nights. We managed to scrape enough together to get by. Still, I remember one winter when we children came down with a very high fever, our mother half-sick herself, hovering over us with a little food or drink till she too went down with the fever. . . .

In 1919, after the Revolution, with all the upheaval and turbulence it produced, the Zielony pogrom came to Pereyaslav. The Zielonys were composed of the lowest criminals. Their motto was: "Beat the Jews; save Russia." Of course, they did not stop with beating and plundering; they killed and maimed young and old, pregnant women and babes in arms. For four days the carnage continued. When the Zielonys departed, there was mourning in many Jewish homes. The unfortunate people who escaped with their lives but were tortured and beaten told horrendous tales. By a stroke of good luck, we were intact physically, but the experience left an indelible mark on my memory. In fact, for years I have been suppressing the thoughts, in order to be able to lead a normal existence.

Somehow, we made it through the year 1920, against all odds. Then, one Saturday in 1921, when it looked the darkest and all hope was dimming of ever reaching the U.S.A., at the synagogue Grandfather Jacob had brought us to and which we attended especially on the Sabbath and holy days, we saw and read a Jewish newspaper. It was printed in the United States, where American Jewish citizens were looking for their families, should they have survived the war and the Revolution. Among those Americans was my father, Simon Knoppow, who was searching for his wife, Chernia, and their five children. . . .

Exhibit B

[On her way to the United States, Sonia met and fell in love with Herbert Michelson (the t was added later), an agent for the White Star Line. In 1924, Herbert joined Sonia in Detroit. She married him later that year and soon was caring for their three children. In 1934, the family moved to Los Angeles to seek treatment for Marvin's sister May, severely stricken with polio (she is now a teacher of the handicapped and a successful artist). Herbert died in 1947, and the next year Sonia's daughters were married in a double ceremony. That left Sonia alone with Marvin, who remained at home till 1950. In a recent letter to her daughters, Sonia described the unusually close relationship that developed between mother and son during those years together.]

Believe me when I state that I do love all of you, my dear children, from the depths of my heart, and that no sacrifice could be too big to make things easier in any way for each of you.

Still [after Herbert's passing and the weddings], I would have felt completely alone if not for the fact that Marvin was with me, and that I still had a big job ahead of me, to guide and help Marvin to obtain a good education, a means to an independent life.

[To support them, Sonia took a job managing a complex of sixty-six apartments.]

Marvin saw how hard I was working, forging ahead more for him than for myself. We worked against great odds.

[While trying to rest up before a friend's bar mitzvah, Sonia accidentally overdosed on a sleeping compound.]

When Dr. Bilon came to see me at the hospital, he asked me, "Sonia, why did you do it?" I looked him straight in the eye and said, "Dr. Bilon, how can you think I would attempt something this foolish while Marvin is in law school?"

[Marvin graduated and was preparing for the bar exam.]

I was sound asleep after an especially grueling day at work, having covered at least several miles and untold numbers of steps. All of a sudden, someone was sobbing. I opened my eyes—Marvin was on his knees beside my bed, weeping aloud, "Mother, my shoulder is in pain; I cannot write anymore."

In the morning, Marvin was to start the bar exam, where he had to write for eight hours. . . . I calmed Marvin down as best I could and we went down to a neighborhood clinic for help. The doctor there said, "Young man, the best advice I can give you is to apply hot compresses." We went home. I kept applying hot compresses for a long time, while Marvin was sound asleep.

Marvin took the exam but he did not make it on his

first try. It was up to me to encourage him again. All I had between me and complete poverty were five $1,000 bonds, but I told him, "Marvin, the bonds will go for the completion of your education, no matter how long it takes." There it was decided.

I cashed the bonds. Marvin went for another six months to law school, took the bar exam once more, and waited impatiently for the results. So did I.

One Saturday in December, Marvin decided to clean the basement. I was in the apartment and happened to see the mailman depositing a long envelope in my mailbox. I quickly snatched the envelope, locked myself in the bathroom, and opened the envelope—to absorb the first shock if the results were unfavorable. Joy of joys—Marvin had made it. With shaking feet I went down to the basement, where Marvin was working, waved the envelope, and said, "Marvin, you are an attorney."

When he heard the news, Marvin sprawled himself on the floor, half sobbing and half laughing, and said, "Mother, we made it. We made it." At that moment, I was fully repaid for all my efforts on Marvin's behalf.

Exhibit C

[By 1979, Marvin was a world-famous attorney. But he still visited his mother every Sunday. Most of the time, Sonia made dinner for him, then took the telephone off the hook so he could catch up on his sleep.

On one such visit, Sonia handed him this letter.]

You are now an accomplished, well-known, highly respected attorney, responsible for several important laws. You have built a very desirable practice. All big pluses. Nonetheless, you have paid a high price for your success. It grieves me very much because you are careless with your health. My guidance and counsel in this respect seem to have fallen on deaf ears. You eat poorly, either too much or too little, and you are always short of time, racing to make one more speech, one more headline. Believe me, Marvin, fame is very fleeting.

You have arrived, Marvin; you can afford to slow down. Rearrange your hours at the office so you can have time to yourself to relax and enjoy life. Health is precious, and when it goes, no wealth can replace it. My love for you would be fortified if you would take better care of my dear Marvin, whom I love and for whom no sacrifice is too big for his mother.

Exhibit D

[In 1983, the British Broadcasting Company began filming a series of programs on the history of the Jews in America. After meeting Sonia, the BBC producers elected to make her one of the stars of the series. They interviewed her extensively about her experiences and even filmed a "typical" Friday night dinner at Sonia's apartment overlooking the Pacific Ocean; what was typical was that Sonia had prepared enough food for an army. But the highlight of the show was a return to Ellis Island, Sonia's "birthplace" as an American sixty-one years before. All three of her children accompanied her to New York (where a year before Sonia had suffered a serious heart attack), rose with her at four in the morning, and joined her on a tugboat hired by the BBC. They sailed toward Ellis Island as the sun came up behind the New York skyline. A few weeks later, Sonia's daughter Marion, a prolific writer, shared her memories in a lengthy and moving letter.]

There was such an air of expectancy for all of us as we chugged our way into the harbor, past the pilings and piers, past the ferryboats docked and waiting to carry the morning commuters to and from Staten Island. The waters were golden, reflecting the morning sky shimmering with the promise of the new day. The mood of anticipation heightened as we continued toward the Statue of Liberty. Appropriately for our mood and purpose, at that early hour the lady's torch was still lit up, which added to the drama.

We could now discern a small island with low buildings scattered over it. Nothing impressive at a distance, but quite foreboding as we drew closer.

We kept watching Mother, to see if she found anything familiar in the buildings, but there was no recognition yet. Nor was there any as we clambered off the tugboat and made our way along the tree-shaded walkway, or as we walked slowly up the stairs and into the reception building. Then Sonia started to cry, suddenly overwhelmed with sadness by the thought that her mother and two of her brothers, who were all young and very much alive when she was last here, have now long since departed.

Again and again, Sonia was prodded to remember her feelings on arriving at this place sixty-one years earlier. Her answers focused repeatedly on two things: how young she was—only twenty—and her feelings of hope. She spoke several times of "the young Sonia" and "the old Sonia"— clearly, she was visualizing herself as she had been, how she had looked, as well as how she had felt. She remembered much more about how she had felt in that place than how the place itself had looked.

She kept saying, "I am only twenty, and I feel hopeful —hopeful about starting a new life."

Exhibit E

[Sonia died shortly after I met her, in December 1984. At the end of her memoirs, Sonia offered this summation of her life.]

My losses were harsh and heavy. . . .
Nevertheless, my gains were considerable. . . .
I admit humbly that my balance sheet is fair.

Bob Dylan's mother

BEATTY RUTMAN

"I DON'T THINK HE WAS EVER THE GREATEST SINGER. HE WAS NEVER AN OPERA STAR."

For Beatrice (Beatty) Rutman, perhaps the most poignant reminder of her status as Bob Dylan's mother came during her grandson Jesse's bar mitzvah in Israel. It was Beatty's idea to have the ceremony at the Wailing Wall. "I was taking a vacation with him anyway. Jesse was seventeen. His younger brothers had both been bar mitzvahed. So I said, 'Why don't you do it?' " In Jerusalem, Beatty and Jesse were joined by Bob, who flew over for the occasion. Also there, but not invited, was a photographer who insisted on taking a shot of Jesse praying. "I begged him not to do it," recalls Beatty. "I said, 'Can't you just leave this boy alone? Doesn't he have a right? Do you have to do this, just to make a few dollars?' But he took the picture anyway, and he wired it to New York, and it made all the papers. So then the whole world knew Jesse Dylan had been bar mitzvahed."

At seventy, Beatty Rutman is used to such intrusions. After all, her son is the most influential singer-songwriter of the rock era (he has sold more than 30 million records) and an enigmatic figure who many fans regarded as a prophet of his generation. No wonder the media's interest in Dylan has been intensive and nonstop. And since Bob himself has carefully avoided interviews for most of his career, frustrated reporters have often turned to Beatty.

Bob's mother has rarely obliged them. "My late husband,

Abe Zimmerman [Bob's father], used to say, 'You read the paper, then you put it in the fireplace.' They write what they want to write. What are you going to do, sue them? I knew Elvis Presley personally, and unfortunately, I think he really cared about what they said about him in the papers. The media have made some people crazy—Bobby was smart enough to stay away from that."

Still, Beatty was willing to speak for publication when reached by phone in St. Paul, Minnesota (where she lived with her husband of fifteen years, Joe Rutman, until his recent death). And she was willing to talk about the period, from 1979 to 1983, when the press was saying that Bob had turned into a Bible-thumping Christian. "He never displayed it for me," she says. But then Beatty adds, "What religion a person is shouldn't make any difference to anybody else. I'm not bigoted in any way. Rabbis would call me up. I'd say, 'If you're upset, you try to change him.' "

Now, by all accounts, Bob is more actively Jewish than ever. On his most recent tour, he caused complications by refusing to perform on shabbes. In the past few years, he has spent time with Hasidic rebbes in Brooklyn, given money to Jewish causes, and made several trips to Israel, including the one for Jesse's bar mitzvah. Of that ceremony, Beatty says, "It was magnificent. It was the high point of my life."

Most of her life was spent in Hibbing, Minnesota, where the family moved when Bob was six. Abe Zimmerman had an appliance store, and Beatty was a popular figure in town. "All these years later," she says, "I can't walk down the street there without everybody stopping me to say hello."

There was no anti-Semitism in Hibbing, according to Beatty. "I got on with everyone. When a Christian friend died, they wanted to have the wake in my house, instead of in a funeral home. I said, 'Okay, but I don't serve ham.' So I made tuna salad and egg salad, and everyone was happy."

Life got interesting when Bobby reached adolescence. He had been a quiet, introspective boy; Beatty says she expected him to become an English teacher. But at ten he started playing the guitar, and soon Bob Dylan—he renamed himself for Dylan Thomas—was carrying his guitar from college campus to college campus, where he found both an audience and a reason to avoid going to high school. His mother was alternately angry and admiring. "There were lots of times when he was ready to come back to Minnesota," Beatty recalls. "But he stuck with it. No one helped Bobby—they shut doors in his face, but no one helped him." She watched his progress from afar—"and then, when he was ready for Carnegie Hall, he called us."

Beatty never expected him to become the success he is; she marvels that "he's so big, and he seems to be getting even bigger."

Beatty says she gets along "very, very well" with Bob and his younger brother, David. "I did a wonderful job raising both my children," she says, "and I've been able to stay close by never interfering."

Does she like Bob's music? "He's a beautiful poet. I have things he wrote for me when he was five or six, sacred things, that I'll never show anyone. But I don't think he was ever the greatest singer. He was never an opera star."

Then she adds, "Of course, I love everything he does. I'm his mother." And what's more, "He's a remarkable, wonderful man. He's a very ordinary person; he's full of compassion; he has no ego. People don't really know him. But I do, and I'm grateful for it. Every mother should have a son like Bobby."

About the author's mother

While I was writing this book, my mother told a friend of hers about it.

"Are you getting a chapter?" asked my mother's friend.

"A chapter? I'll be lucky if I get a paragraph," answered my mother.

When she told me this story, she added, "And I deserve a chapter. Is it my fault you're not famous?"

No, Mom, it's not your fault. So here's your chapter.

Marilyn Bernstein was born Marilyn Weinberg in the Bronx —back when the Bronx was a great place to grow up. "We had skating season; we had marbles season; we had jump-rope season," she remembered. "There were so few cars, you could spend hours playing in the street. And they kept the schoolyard open, even in the summer."

But her own home wasn't such a fun place to be.

Marilyn's parents were poor. Her father, Nat, who came over from Poland with his parents and nine brothers before World War I, was a cutter of ladies' garments. During the Depression, he was out of work as much as he was at work. About the only good thing about being unemployed was that it gave him time to help his brother, Jack, open a hardware store. Jack made lots of money. Nat never did.

Rebecca, my mother's mother, also arrived at Ellis Island as a child. She was one of seven sisters. Her father, Samuel Goldman, was a shammes—a caretaker of a synagogue—in the Bronx. My mother remembered his Passover seders—with dozens of aunts, and uncles, and cousins crowded around the holiday table.

By the time she was thirteen, Marilyn and her friends were taking the double-decker buses down Fifth Avenue on weekends. Movies cost a dime then—and they came with newsreels, serials, and a stageshow. Sometimes she went with her big brother, Eli.

At fourteen, Marilyn had to go to work. Her first job was at S. Klein, picking dresses off the floor and putting them on hangers. At sixteen she became a secretary at the Robbins Music Company. That was a little more interesting. Frank Sinatra and Dean Martin often came by the office, and Irving Caesar, who wrote the songs "Tea for Two" and "Swanee," took her out for her first steak.

At night, Marilyn went to the movies or the theater with friends—then they *walked* home to the Bronx, stopping at the Eclair on West Seventy-second Street for pastries. The friends she made during that era—"career girls" like Bertha Schwartz and Alita Hernandez—remained her friends for life. Mom was so good at keeping friends that I used to think she had more of them than anyone I knew.

Marilyn defied her parents by taking her own apartment, in Chelsea, when she was twenty-three. It was the first time she had had her own room. She also scandalized the family by taking trips alone—including one to Mexico, by train. But she returned to New York and met Milton Bernstein, a handsome young accountant, at a movie. When she broke her leg on an icy sidewalk, Milton cared for her, and they became engaged a few weeks later.

After they married, Marilyn and Milton lived in her old neighborhood in the Bronx. But when their first child, Elizabeth, was three—and just a week before "Freddy" was born—they moved to Queens. Marilyn learned to drive; she was the first member of her family to do so. Six years later, the family moved to a split-level house in Jericho, Long Island. She was the first member of her family to own a home.

Marilyn threw herself into suburban life. She drove her husband to the railroad station every morning, became a den mother when Fred wanted to join the Cub Scouts, and learned to do the fix-it jobs the super had always done for them in the Bronx.

The schools in Jericho were great, and both children thrived. Elizabeth was a brilliant student who went to Cornell at sixteen, and then to Harvard Law School. Fred was editor of his school paper, and he was on the TV show *It's Academic* (the team lost when Fred couldn't remember that the U.S. coin worth one dollar and made of silver is called—time's up!—the silver dollar).

It must have been the only time he was ever tongue-tied. Fred, a nonstop talker, was a difficult child to raise. But Marilyn raised him well—with patience and devotion.

When her children were in school, Marilyn went back to work. With the first spare cash she'd ever had, she rediscovered her love of traveling. She went to London with Milton, and she went to Athens with a friend. And she went to Israel with Milton and a friend—and met a lot of relatives she never even knew existed.

Then, the week Fred started Princeton—which meant she'd finally have some peace and quiet—Marilyn discovered she had cancer. She fought it valiantly, braving surgery, radiation therapy, and two years of numbing chemotherapy treatments.

When the disease went into remission, she continued working and she continued traveling. Marilyn from the Bronx became a regular in Tuba City, Arizona (where Liz had moved to become a lawyer for the Navajo tribe), and Los Angeles, California, where Fred, by now a *People* magazine reporter, took her to all the hot spots.

She encouraged her kids—even when they chose careers that might have seemed offbeat. "I want it to go on record," she jokingly told a friend of mine, "that I never pushed Fred to become a doctor."

She should have. It might have helped to have another ally in the war against her cancer. When the disease came back, she resumed struggling. She even made a wedding for Liz (who married fellow lawyer John MacKinnon) and moved from her house in Jericho to a city apartment between chemotherapy treatments, in order to start a new life.

Marilyn did a lot of struggling. Now she's finally getting some rest.